SEAWEED IN THE KITCHEN

Himalanthia elongata (Sea Spaghetti)

THE COASTLINE KITCHEN

SEAWEED IN THE KITCHEN

Fiona Bird

PROSPECT BOOKS

2019

Edible seaweeds in the lower shore with all three major groups: green (Sea Lettuce, Ulva spp.), brown (Kelp, Laminaria and Sea Spaghetti, Himanthalia), and red (Dulse, Palmaria growing on stipes).

First published in 2015 in Great Britain and the United States
by Prospect Books,
26 Parke Road, London, SW13 9NG

Revised edition printed in 2019

BRITISH LIBRARY CATALOGUING IN PUBLICATION DATA:
A catalogue entry of this book is available from the British Library.

Typeset and designed by Catheryn Kilgarriff and Brendan King in Adobe Garamond Pro.

Cover design by Prospect Books.

ISBN 978-1-909248-39-7

Printed and bound by the Gutenberg Press, Malta.

CONTENTS

This revised publication is dedicated to Professor Michael D Guiry. Thank you for answering my many questions speedily and assuring me that 'no question is silly'.

ACKNOWLEDGEMENTS

On the island of South Uist I am surrounded by deserted white beaches and aquamarine seas, and so it is unsurprising that I chose to eat and write about sea vegetables over terrestrial vegetables, which have spent hours on a ferry boat. In writing this book, I have stumbled upon a cornucopia of delightful seaweed enthusiasts from academics, who replied to my excited emails, to food writers such as Catherine Phipps, whose children, Lilly and Adam now request 'more seaweed please'. My support list is long but must begin with my mother, Joy Murray, who feeds seaweed biscuits to her friends, and Stephen, Xander, Jhonti, Lili, Alasdair, Xavier and Maxim to whom I owe a tangle of thanks for eating seaweed at every available opportunity, even in porridge at breakfast. Seaweed rocks and so do you all. My thanks go, therefore, to: Alex Adrian, Juliet Brodie, Dr Matthew Dalby, Mike Guiry, Tom Devine, Gavin Hardy, Sarah Hotchkiss, Alan Imeson, Pete Moore, Ole Mouritsen, Leonel Pereira, Craig Rose, Anne Secord, Jennifer Sharp, Dr Duncan Smallman, Magimix UK, and to Catheryn Kilgarriff for the opportunity to revisit the text. For permission to use their recipes I must also thank Elizabeth Bird, John Lewis-Stempel, Dr Alice Liu, Elisabeth Luard, Jade Mellor, Catherine Phipps, and Inver Restaurant, Cairndow, Argyll. And last but not least, my thanks to Tom Jaine for giving me the opportunity to swim with seals (which I still loathe), to stumble upon the Victorian seaweed sisterhood, and to share my passion for seaweed.

Red rags – false dulse (Dilsea carnosa)

INTRODUCTION

Seaweed is on the Islander's seascape but has demanded little British interest until more recent times. However, as long ago as 1842, the phycologist or studier of seaweed Amelia Griffiths grumbled to Miles Berkeley, author of *Gleanings of British Algae*, that no one in Torquay could identify seaweeds but all accepted them willingly as good for manure. However, a large number of Victorian ladies could name any amount of flowers, ferns or fungus and many clergymen had ambitions to follow in the footsteps of the out-of-doors naturalist Gilbert White, a clergyman and author of *The Natural History of Selborne* (published in 1789).

Seaweed, which has been the friend of the farmer and gardener for centuries, is nutrient rich but also high in water and is classified by colour. The reds and greens (*Rhodophyceae* and *Chlorophyceae*) belong in the plant kingdom, and the browns (*Phaeophyceae*) belong in the kingdom of *Chromista*, which include some fungi, water moulds and the phytoplankton group of diatoms. Perhaps due to their evolution (not belonging to the plant kingdom), brown seaweeds tend to be much larger than the red and and green seaweeds, but all provide habitat and food source to marine life.

Red seaweeds
Kingdom *Plantae*
Phylum *Rhodophyta*
Classes *Bangiophyceae* and *Florideophyceae*

Green seaweeds
Kingdom *Plantae*
Phylum *Chlorophyta*
Class *Ulvophyceae*

Brown seaweeds
Kingdom *Chromista*
Phylum *Ochrophyta*
Class *Phaeophyceae*

There are about 7,000 species of red seaweeds, 2,000 brown and 1,000 green. That's an awful lot of seaweeds. Sadly, I will only focus on a small number of easily recognized, edible species in this book.

The idea of cooking with seaweed would have been far from the mind of even the most enthusiastic Victorian seaweed collector. Times are changing; today there are numerous exciting seaweed proposals in the offing. The bio fuel industry has seaweed plans that may result in a reduction of our use of fossil fuels, and the cosmetic industry has long realised seaweed's revitalising properties. Seaweed as a source of phycocolloids is an old friend of the chemist and industrial cook. Seaweed polysaccharides (phycocolloids found in alginates, agar and carrageen) are tasteless but have properties that form gels in aqueous solution. They also improve texture and prevent separation. However, kelp is exciting more than *dashi* and Japanese chefs. British kitchens and restaurants are entertaining recipes which include seaweed – and not always in an oriental style.

Wild seaweed and coastal plants have been harvested for food and used in traditional Chinese and herbal medicine for centuries. In early eighth century Japan, seaweeds such as wakame, kelp and nori were noted as a form of taxation payment in an administrative and penal code of the Taihō era, enacted in AD 703. Historically seaweed is well documented as important in the diets of the inhabitants of the Far East and Pacific. The Māori ate species of red and green seaweed, and fashioned brown seaweed kelp into hunting bags. Other countries still uphold aged seaweed customs. An ancient Korean tradition is to serve brown seaweed soup, called *miyeok-guk* to postpartum mothers and on birthdays: Wakame is the key ingredient. Korean folklore suggests that seaweed symbolises rejuvenation because whales eat seaweed after giving birth. I leave this with you. In her book *Korea and Her Neighbours* (1897), the Victorian traveller, Isabella Bird notes Koreans collecting seaweed: 'Seaweed is a common article of diet and is dried and carried everywhere into the interior. I have scarcely seen a coolie make a meal of which it is not a part, either boiled, fried, pickled, raw or in soup.' She also penned that seaweed was the food of peasants who could not afford to eat rice. However, historically it has always been eaten (*miyeok*) so this disputes any suggestion of seaweed as a Korean survival food.

The seaweed Limu kala is important in Hawaiian heritage as a symbol of forgiveness amongst quarrelling families or individuals. Hawaiians eat more than forty species of seaweeds (as do the Polynesians) and as a direct consequence have a large repertoire of seaweed recipes – these are worthy of perusal. In Northern Thailand the fresh water seaweed *Cladophora* known as Kai, is an important green seaweed that is sold in markets. It is used in the kitchen in a similar way to nori. Somewhat conversely in the West, the Classicists' dislike of seaweed is symptomatic of an ancient and widespread European indifference. The Roman poet Virgil (70–19BC) dismissed seaweed as *vilior alga*, which translates as 'vile seaweed'. To those who know the value of marine crops, it seems inconceivable that the useful forms were called sea 'weeds'. Perhaps this is why we now see the use of a more technical word combination marine algae. The general European consensus was that seaweed was for animals or agriculture. However, some European countries, notably Scandinavia, Iceland, Ireland and parts of Scotland and Wales, resisted this negative trend. The American authors Rachel Carson and Euell Gibbons credit immigrant Irish with American street corner sales of dried dulse, which was chewed like tobacco. Also on that continent, dulse with Irish moss or carrageen was an important industry in Prince Edward Island. According to the Icelandic Sagas, *Palmaria palmata* – called 'sol' in Iceland – has been known to be edible since at least the year 961. The Icelanders' oldest law book written in the first half of the twelfth century mentions the right to collect and, in addition, the right to eat sol when on another man's land, which means that sol was also eaten fresh. The right to collect sol was considered a great concession and licenses were issued to many churches all around Iceland. References relating to events happening in 1118 mention the collecting of, and trading with, sol. It was a common Icelandic victual and one which coastal harvesters exchanged for wool and meat. Sol was dried in huts and was highly valued as a healthy and nourishing food. In the main, however, in Europe seaweed was associated with poverty and eaten with reluctance, during times of food shortage. Lack of Western seaweed culinary knowledge may in part be attributed to it being considered a poor man's food. The existence of a Scottish consultation paper is, however, evidence that the tide is turning and seaweed is a subject worthy of discussion. Scottish Natural Heritage has appointed a designated seaweed officer, and seaweed has moved well beyond sushi in the kitchens of British chefs.

In its quest for healthier food, the British food industry is using seaweed as a low salt alternative. Meanwhile a study at Hallam Sheffield University noted that when knotted wrack is added to wholemeal bread dough, its shelf life is extended. Delving further, there are plenty of references to seaweed in industrial and manufactured products. It helps ice cream to slide down our throats and is in the paste that every good child puts on a toothbrush before they go to bed. Seaweed, albeit disguised, is on the British shopping list.

We live in a hectic world, where food is available 24/7 and its preparation often demands minimal fuss and effort. Gathering wild food doesn't work like this. Even coastal dwellers with a cornucopia of seaweeds and plants on their doorstep, may not have the time or inclination to gather free ingredients. Time is precious. Hard core foragers may grind acorns for flour, but many British cooks associate wild food with possible toxicity. Some children aren't familiar with where and how common cooking ingredients are grown, so the idea of cooking green and slimy seaweed is anathema. Parents and children alike need to be gently coaxed into the mysterious world of seaweed, where some species may in fact be red or brown, as well as green. Those who have already considered cooking with seaweed may have been hampered by the scarcity of decent recipes. Little has been written on the subject of eating British seaweed. Traditional ideas tend to concentrate on the red seaweeds: dulse, laver and carrageen. The instruction of recipes that do exist is often far from didactic. However, on the plus side, wild plants and seaweeds aren't grown in poly-tunnels (yet) and remain seasonal in the original sense of the word. Seaweed has a growing season too, although because the study of seaweed (phycology) is in its infancy, there is much for academics to learn.

I live on an island with a lacework of lochans and rocky and sandy coastlines. Seaweed is prolific and provides free food for my kitchen table. In spring, gathering seaweed with the sun on my back as I clamber over rocks banked with pink Sea Thrift, is a privilege, but one that can be shared. With foraging comes time to appreciate the natural beauty of our British coast. Whilst searching for wild food, the coastal forager can reflect upon his or her thoughts until perhaps a noisy oystercatcher, gull or badly judged incoming wave interrupts the silence. More often than not, foragers have a sense of stealth and slowness about them and an overwhelming sense of the moment. The hunter-gatherer may press on fuelled by optimistic hope, but ingredients for his or her supper can never be guaranteed. Each year brings gluts and famines even to the seasoned gatherer who knows the local patch. The forager understands the meaning of slow food but also the swiftness of each passing season. The weather may be helpful or at times cruel and mulishly unrelenting. Coastal foragers have an added conundrum for they must learn to understand and work in partnership with the rhythm of the sea.

Different species of seaweed grow in each tidal zone as you step from the sea-splashed cliffs to the lowest tidewater mark. In Britain the range of tides is great, which makes seaweed foraging very exciting. The Bristol Channel (the Severn Bore) has the third largest tidal range in the world, boasting spring tidal ranges of up to 10 metres. A British seaweed collector will become conscious of the daily, hourly change of the ebb and flow of seawater. No two days are the same. The sea doesn't rest, its move is constant and the moon dictates its high and low water marks. The period between each high and low tide is 12 hours and 25 minutes, which means that the tidal cycle is a little later each day. Seasoned seaweed cooks who live by the sea, will often have a tide clock in their kitchen. My dog's walk usually coincides with low tide so that I can pick seaweed, unless of course the hour is dark and uncivilised. After a full or new moon the forces acting on the sea are stronger than at other times of the month. This is because the sun and moon are directly in line with the earth. It causes the greatest difference in tides and happens over the days immediately following the full or new moon. These tides are known as spring tides, when the tides rise higher and lower than at any other time. At the quarter moon the interaction of the forces of the sun and moon interfere with each other and this produces sluggish neap tides, where there is a less marked difference between high and low water marks. The word neap is perhaps Norse in origin, where it means forked. This would make sense because at a neap tide, the sun and moon are angled. The author Rachel Carson says that neap is of Scandinavian origin and that it means barely touching. Either way, neap tides are somewhat lethargic in their ability to cover the extremes of the foreshore.

A perigee moon appears bigger and brighter than other moons because the moon has reached the point in its orbit when it is closest to the earth. The days following these super moons and the equinoxes, when Northern and Southern Hemispheres are equally illuminated, bring very low spring tides. These are red-letter days in a seaweed collector's calendar. Picking seaweed at the low waters of neap tides is far less exciting. The true intertidal zone however, is probably best described as the area between the high and low neap tide marks, where the shore is covered and uncovered daily by the tide.

The space revealed at low tides is magical. The dimension of the ocean's secret garden is never the same on two consecutive days, and the ethereal nature and variation of its contents makes it compulsive viewing. Even flotsam cast by man harbours visitors. You may even spy goose barnacles, which were mentioned in John Gerard's *Herball, or Generall Historie of Plantes* (1597). Gerard wrongly suggested that they were destined to become barnacle geese due to their feathery covering. Other man-made flotsam homes the ubiquitous barnacle clad mussels. For the seaweed collector the relationship between the tides and beach zones will become clearer as he or she becomes familiar with species of seaweeds. Suddenly a definite and obvious pattern of growth will become clear. Some seaweed thrives on rocky or sandy coastline but all flourish in the tidal rhythm of the sea. Knotted wrack is long and slender with air bubbles or bladders that prefer a protected shore, a beach that surfers wouldn't care to visit. Bladder wrack has pairs of bladders down a sturdy mid-rib and this can adapt to rougher surf. At times bladder wrack swells and looks almost heart-shaped. It's a reproductive thing. The hardier seaweeds such as channel wrack can withstand long periods out of water between tides (desiccation) and as a consequence inhabit the upper beach zone. As you wander down to the sea, this member of the wrack family looks black and brittle but once sprayed with seawater, it regains colour and texture. The green seaweeds (*Chlorophyceae*) are found on the upper shore and in the intertidal zone, where there is plenty of sunlight. The red seaweeds (*Rhodophyceae*) are a light sensitive bunch because their pigment composition is such that it usually requires a layer of water between it and the sun. The red group is only visible at very low tides. The browns (*Phaeophyceae*) are so coloured because they contain pigments, which conceal their greenness or chlorophyll. Rather confusingly some brown members may appear as olive green or yellow. This may all sound like a school biology revision lesson but to the seaweed collector it will become common sense. The naming of species of seaweed is confusing too; on occasion academic re-classification involves a change in the Latin, botanical name. The first person to name a seaweed is also noted in its Latin classification. For example dabberlocks (*Alaria esculenta*)*,* was noted by Robert Kaye Greville in his *Algae Britannicae* of 1830, but Linnaeus was the first to describe the seaweed itself in 1767 under the name *Fucus esculenta*. This is why it is written in taxonomies as '*Alaria esculenta* (Linnaeus) Greville 1830'. I was intrigued by the use of the Latin word for food, *esculenta*. Linnaeus' influence was great. D.H. Stoever (his first biographer) described him as the most systematical genius of the age. It was Linnaeus who first persuaded the world of natural historians that providing every distinct organism with a name was the foundation of scientific understanding. Fortunately he developed his binomial (two-name) system, in which each living thing is given a name consisting of two Latin words, at a time when there was a popular interest in natural history. The first word is the name of the genus and the second the species. The reference system devised by Linnaeus, who is often referred to as the 'Father of Systematic Botany', is an inclusive plan, understood in all languages. He used Latin because it was the custom of his age. However, had he used Swedish, his native tongue, he would have made little impact. Linnaeus' brilliance was to devise a classification system and nomenclature for the whole natural world which triumphed over all rivals. The Victorian seaside ladies (of whom I will speak much) and gentlemen benefited hugely from this. Dr Anne Secord says that Linnaeus was very interested in foodstuffs and diet. Indeed in Lisbet Koerner's book *Linnaeus: Nature and Nation*, Linnaeus recommends that the starving poor of Sweden ate seaweed amongst other wild edibles. In general, I shall refer to edible seaweed and wild plants by their common names. Professor Mike Guiry suggests that 'Life was simple when all green-coloured algae were included in a single class, the *Chlorophyceae.*' He says that progress has been so rapid that textbooks are out of date almost as soon as they are printed. Those interested in precise classification should refer to Guiry's website Algaebase, which is updated regularly.

An exposed rocky shore at low tides will reveal magnificent red, green or brown seaweeds, but as the tide rises the crashing waves will quickly fill the rock pools where earlier the seaweed forager paddled confidently. An ebbing tide is more restful and will comfort a timid forager because it lacks the thrust of the incoming wave. The sea is omnipotent, and even when it appears calm and at rest it is in control and will dictate the seaweed collector's schedule.

Small fishing boats anchored on a sandy bay at low tide are within pedestrian reach but as the tide turns, stormy, white seahorses may spray the decks of the boats and the ocean's sandy carpet will vanish. The punctual tide doesn't await either the fisherman or seaweed gatherer. Listening to the susurration of gentle waves on a warm day whilst I harvest seaweed is a simple pleasure. At other less clement times, the icy drench of a crashing wave is rewarded in the kitchen, because there the seaweed releases an ocean secret. Some call it umami. Dining on seaweed which you've harvested, prepared and cooked yourself is an ocean-to-plate experience. The novice seaweed gatherer may look smugly upon the hunter of fungi because a toxic seaweed is rare. The brown algae *Desmarestia spp* releases sulphuric acid when picked, but identify this species as one to avoid, and the foreshore is clear. Some marine algae don't taste very nice, and such seaweeds are not included in my recipes.

Anyone collecting wild food should harvest safely and sustainably. In the case of seaweed this means leaving the holdfast. A holdfast is similar to the roots of a plant, but as the word suggests it secures the seaweed to its growing place. This may be a huge rock or a tiny cowrie shell (which is beautiful in its own right and has been collected for centuries).

The amber kelps grow in dark subtidal forests that are occasionally exposed at exceptional low spring tides. These forests are every bit as spectacular as any terrestrial forest, although only a privileged few have really seen them. However, the vast majority of algae are small and inconspicuous. To view their beauty and diversity often requires a magnifying glass or microscope. The holdfasts of the larger kelps remind me of the crooked roots of an old tree. The kelps have strong stipes or stalks which support their branching slippery fronds (think plant leaves). Giant kelps are often thrown ashore after a storm, and although at first sight they look similar, each has its own definite character. The sugar kelp frond reminds me of the tail of the mermaid in the Hans Christian Andersen tale. It is often covered in a white sugary substance called mannitol. Its frond may cover metres, but I advise the novice cook to seek out younger specimens. Some sugar kelp fronds are shorter than its stipe. Fresh sugar kelp cooks quickly and is an excellent choice for the apprentice seaweed cook. The *Laminarias* or kelp forests appear dark and forbidding but in their tangled underwater jungle there is order. The seaweed gatherer will first pass oarweed (*L. digitata*) and then, on wading or swimming further out, forest kelp (or cuvie, *L. hyperborea*). The kelp forests provide homes to fauna and seaweed epiphytes like dulse, which hitches a ride on rough stipes. At high tide the larger stipes are reminiscent of the guards at Buckingham Palace, as they stand to underwater attention. The slippery kelp fronds dance and provide shelter for

Forest kelp *(Laminaria hyperborea)*

darting fish playing hide and seek. Kelp also hosts lunch, supper or tea for many invertebrates, such as the blue ray limpet. But then twice a day, when the tide retreats, the party is halted as the seaweed collapses and falls flat on the seabed. Some seaweeds lie upon sand and others hang from the rocks or droop, as is the case for the kelp *L. digitata*, which unlike *L hyperborea* has a flexible stipe. But all await the surge of water which will once again hold larger stipes erect, and enable the seaweed fronds to flap and return to the marine ball.

The sustainability of wild seaweed is a topical issue but it was ever thus. The Victorians were avid collectors of seaweed and are held responsible for giving it some delightful colloquial names. Professor Juliet Brodie of the British Natural History Museum speculates that Victorian seaweed collectors had a far greater impact on reducing the distribution of some of the more charismatic seaweeds, such as peacocks tail (*Padina pavonica*), than the environmental forces that seaweeds are subjected to today. Peacocks tail is stunning. I'm not surprised that it was a collector's item. The seaweed code, as with any wild food, is: forage only where seaweed is prolific, keep up to date with current research (growing points), cut well above the holdfast (think plant root) and take enough for yourself and no more. For the landlocked or busy, dried seaweed and edible coastal plants are readily available in shops or from a commercial forager. Payment spares a wet seaside adventure and in the case of seaweed, its subsequent washing, drying or freezing. For those with limited time to visit the coast, drying or freezing captures holiday adventures in a jar or container, and is very easy to do. Further instruction will follow in a later chapter. Wild coastal ingredients are available from licensed professional foragers, and increasingly in the supermarket aisles. The seaweed capsule in the herbal chemist may be labelled as highly nutritious, but so is cooking and eating seaweed. Personally, I think that it's more pleasurable to eat seaweed than to take it in tablet form. I enjoy foraging seaweed, but the recipes in this book will work equally well with shop purchased ingredients. The tasting experience isn't limited.

My recipes use seaweeds which are local to me. Make your seaweed choice to suit geography, access and palate. Research into how the nutrients found in seaweed are digested by humans is ongoing, but research on the horizon appears to be seaweed friendly. Think big flavour, like bacon, that is inclusive and for sharing. Seaweed is vegetarian and vegan friendly too. Learn to trust your palate, not just to rely on the recipe or instructions on the seaweed packet. Weirdly, on occasion, you may need to add salt, in spite of having used an ingredient that thrives in seawater. The first time you taste seaweed you may be blown away by the umami, fifth taste factor, but as a seaweed cook you'll learn to be discerning. The journey is personal. Vary the species, gather sparingly, a little here and there, and experiment because to date the research is somewhat sketchy. This collection of recipes is here to stimulate your imagination and taste, rather than provide proscriptive instruction. Blend seaweeds as you gain in culinary confidence, but do so with care, for each has its own distinctive flavour. Potatoes, lamb and eggs are simple beginner's ingredients that guarantee a delicious partnership as you begin a seaweed voyage. 'When the tide goes out the table is laid.'

From early spring to autumn there is an assortment of succulent, wild vegetables available for anyone to pick as they walk down to the beach. Wild ingredients hide in the crevices of cliffs, in sand dunes and tidal flats, all of which are splashed or bathed in salt water. Inexperienced coastal foragers must take a pocket guide to help with identification. On returning home, and before cooking anything, cross-reference foraged ingredients with a book that is far too heavy to put in a rucksack. Foraging courses are useful, as are well-seasoned wild food friends. The same pattern should be followed when you pick seaweed for cooking. The wild green sorrel, which our predecessors used in place of lemon, is one of the first spring greens to put in an appearance. As the months progress, other wild edibles such as glasswort and rock samphire poke up through the sand and mud. These wild ingredients have roots rather than holdfasts but where fitting, they are the focus of recipes in this book.

During recent decades rates of obesity and type 2 diabetes have increased, and it is often argued that the Second World War rationed diet is a healthy, food choice model. This suggests that we should explore eating less rather than plenty on demand, to relieve the burgeoning NHS budget. Preindustrial hunter-gatherers were probably less prone to famines than agriculturalists because they weren't tethered to the land and could, when necessary, move on. The feast and famine issue is frequently applied to wild ingredients but I'd like to think that our forbearers were sensible enough to eat the glut, rather than fret over ingredients that were unavailable. One of the latest diets is the Paleolithic, or 'Paleo' for those in the know. It is loosely based around meats, fish, eggs, vegetables, fruits, nuts and seeds, which were the foods eaten by stone age hunter gatherers. Instead of ruminating over – and I use that word deliberately because paleo animals are grass fed – what we can or can't eat, we should go outside and reacquaint ourselves with wild edibles. Previous generations used wild ingredients in the kitchen as a normal course of culinary event, without thought of wild adventures. During the years of the Second World War, the Ministry of Food encouraged people to forage and cook with wild ingredients. A recipe for rosehip syrup is in a wartime government pamphlet. Rosehips are free and rich in Vitamin C. When you pick wild ingredients in their natural setting you are aware of the root, or indeed the holdfast, of your food. Through this knowledge, gatherers of wild food become better caretakers of the environment. Over picking isn't an issue because those in touch with the land and sea have had jam, have jam and want to ensure that there is jam tomorrow, unlike poor Alice in Wonderland. It's not too late for the generation raised on manufactured food that is always pressed for time to slow down, to take the sea air and taste the real flavour of beach ingredients.

In the words of the poet Lord Byron: 'There is a rapture on the lonely shore, There is society, where none intrudes, By the deep sea, and music in its roar: I love not man the less, but Nature more.'

Osmundea pinnatifida (Pepper Dulse)

Intertidal of St Kilda in the sun. On the left, wracks (Fucus) drying in the sun; on the right laver (Pyropia/Porphyra) lying invitingly on gutweed

CHAPTER ONE

GATHERING SEAWEED ON THE SEASHORE

Under Roman law, the seashore, as far as the waves go out at their furthest point, is considered as belonging to all men.

Today, the Queen owns approximately half of the UK foreshore. This includes the territorial seabed out to 12 nautical miles and beds of tidal rivers. The Crown Estate manages the foreshore for the Sovereign (Crown Estate Act of 1961) and grants licences to those who harvest seaweed commercially from Crown-owned foreshore and/or seabed. The foreshore is legally defined in Halibury's *Laws of England* as the area between mean high water (MHW) and mean low water mark (MLW). In Scotland the foreshore lies between MHW springs and MLW springs, which refers to spring tides when the foreshore is a greater area than during a neap tide. This doesn't apply to Orkney and Shetland, which come under Udal law because they were formerly part of the Norwegian Crown.

In Scotland the owner of the foreshore has exclusive use of taking seaweed and other materials, provided he does nothing to hinder public right of access. In England, Wales and Northern Ireland there is no public right of access at low tide – although there may be a permissive right from the Crown where personal use/access is the intended purpose. A permissive right is when there is a tradition of somebody doing something, along the lines of 'It has always been thus'. Succinctly, permission to forage seaweed should not be taken for granted, you need to find out who owns the foreshore. This may not necessarily be the Crown; it may be the National Trust, RSPB, or indeed a local authority or a landowner. Under normal circumstances, however, unless you are harvesting seaweed commercially or causing a nuisance, it is probably all right to gather a small basket of seaweed. With regard to coastal plants, under common law a forager has the right to pick wild edibles for his or her own consumption. National and local laws may vary, but the Theft Act 1968 is useful, although not applicable to Scotland.

Earlier I discussed the effect that the moon has on the tide, and the high and low watermarks of spring and neap tides. Edward Forbes (1815–1854), a marine naturalist from Douglas on the Isle of Man, was possibly the first person to divide the British coast into depth zones. He named four:

The Littoral Zone, *lying between high and low tidal marks.*

The Laminarian Zone, *from low water to a depth of 7–15 fathoms (13–27 m), dominated by the seaweed Laminaria;*

The Coralline Zone, from 15–30 fathoms (27–90 m), containing the coralline algae in abundance; and

The Zone of Corals, averaging 60 fathoms in depth (90– beyond 100 m), inhabited by the true corals, a region as yet but imperfectly known.

Unfortunately, he published in an obscure journal, so his paper attracted little attention. Philip (Fritz) Rehbock (1942–2002), a historian of marine biology, provided a bibliography of others who published similar studies. In 1957 Joel Hedgpeth sought standardisation of the classification of zones, and noted that although later researchers had adopted Forbes' name of littoral zone, not all limited it to the intertidal zone, and that intertidal would therefore be a clearer term. He rightly highlighted that naming a zone after a common seaweed such as the Laminarian Zone was unsatisfactory for parts of the world where that genus did not exist. Rehbock noted that zones are not immutably fixed according to tidal levels, but tend to spread wider and higher with heavier wave action.

The lunar movements of the tide result in clearly defined zones on the beach. Seaweed species will vary depending on the type of beach and zone. This diagram (right) shows the zones and gives a general idea of where a specie of seaweed is most likely to be found. Tide times vary depending on where you are picking seaweed. A decent local tide timetable is useful, or you can also find times on the internet. A tide times app is available for mobile phones.

Picking and storing seaweeds requires a skill, which comes with practice. In his directions for collecting and preserving seaweeds, William Hooker's instructions ensured the sustained quality of seaweed specimens after extensive travel. Seaweed requires quite different handling to flowering plants. Although Hooker was writing for herbarium collections, his work has some relevance for culinary seaweed collectors today.

Seaweed for cooking should be collected at low tide from a clean beach, well away from fresh water outlets or sewage pipes.

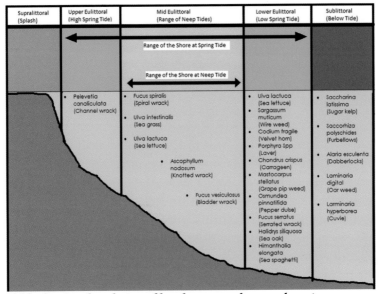

Supralittoral (Splash)	Upper Eulittoral (High Spring Tide)	Mid Eulittoral (Range of Neep Tides)	Lower Eulittoral (Low Spring Tide)	Sublittoral (Below Tide)
		Range of the Shore at Spring Tide		
		Range of the Shore at Neep Tide		
• Pelevetia canaliculata (Channel wrack)	• Fucus spiralis (Spiral wrack) • Ulva intestinalis (Sea grass) • Ulva lactuca (Sea lettuce) • Ascophyllum nodosum (Knotted wrack) • Fucus vesiculosus (Bladder wrack)		• Ulva lactuca (Sea lettuce) • Sargassum muticum (Wire weed) • Codium fragile (Velvet horn) • Porphyra Spp (Laver) • Chondrus crispus (Carrageen) • Mastocarpus stellatus (Grape pip weed) • Osmundea pinnatifida (Pepper dulse) • Fucus serratus (Serrated wrack) • Halidrys siliquosa (Sea oak) • Himanthalia elongata (Sea spaghetti)	• Saccharina latissima (Sugar kelp) • Saccorhiza polyschides (Furbellows) • Alaria esculenta (Dabberlocks) • Laminaria digital (Oar weed) • Larminaria hyperborea (Cuvie)

Table showing the relation of beach zones and seaweed species © Jhonti Bird.

Time your harvest to begin whilst the tide is still going out, to maximize harvesting time. Do not pick storm cast or floating seaweed. Take a small knife or scissors and a separate bag for each species because this will save sorting time in the kitchen. Seal each bag with a freezer tag so that the seaweed retains its moisture. It's useful to record where it was picked and then you can note geographical variations. Pebbles are useful, to weigh down a basket or carrier bag and stop it from blowing away. You need both hands free to pick. A plastic basket or small bucket with tiny holes in the bottom, enables you to rinse picked seaweed in the sea, and later, eases kitchen washing. All seaweed should be rinsed in situ, to enable as many residents as possible to find a new seaside home.

SAFETY ON THE SEASHORE
- There is less risk if you forage with a friend
- If alone tell someone where you propose to forage

- Follow the tide out for safety and to see seaweeds as they uncover
- Be weather and tide aware. Check local forecasts and tide times
- Take a fully charged mobile phone in case of emergency
- Wear non-slip footwear
- Beware of sinking mud estuaries

SUSTAINABILITY

Never cut more than a fifth of the seaweed available and do not pick it unless it is growing prolifically. We have much to learn about the regeneration of seaweed. Sometimes (as with sea spaghetti for example) regrowth is from the frond, so cutting incorrectly will inhibit future growth. Seaweed is part of an ecosystem that other organisms rely on too. It would be prudent to keep up to speed with current scientific research. The internet is a good place to look. There is a concentration on the gelling properties of seaweed, but increasingly regeneration (its growing points) is on the agenda, not least because of the interest in mechanical seaweed dredging. The United Nations FAO publications are also useful (aquaculture). My mantra is: *Forage a little seaweed here and there, and for your own consumption only.* Take care when harvesting invasive seaweeds such as wireweed, and avoid transferring spores to other sites as you forage. Extra care should be taken when harvesting in erosion zones (e.g. sand dunes), because here seaweed acts as a barrier and breaks the force of powerful waves.

CLOTHING

In summer I gather seaweed in as little clothing as possible, and wear jelly shoes to avoid possible injury from the dorsal spines of weaver fish. In winter neoprene gloves, waterproofs and wellington boots are best. Committed seaweed gatherers may like to invest in a wetsuit. This is useful in winter when wayward spray, high waves and cold winds can be unpredictable. It is certainly the warmest clothing option. Although it is more pleasant to harvest in sunshine, on cooler, cloudy days the cut

THE REDS

Latin Name	Common Name	Where it is found	GB Distribution
Porphyra spp	Laver Sloke Black Butter Purple Sea-Vegetable Nori	Rocks and stones Lower and middle shore	UK wide but species specific (see *Porphyra spp*)
Palmaria palmata	Dulse Dillisk Dillease	Attached to rocks and lower shore. Epithetic on kelp *L. hyperborea,* lower shore	UK wide apart
Osmundea osmunda	Royal Fern Weed		UK wide apart
Chondrus crispus *Mastocarpus stellatus* (Grape Pip Weed)	Carrageen Irish Moss Jelly Moss Carragheen Carrageenan Mousse d'Irlande	Intertidal, subtidal *Mastocarpus stellatus* (Grape Pip Weed) is often havested with carrageen, it is rougher but similar	UK wide
Osmundea pinnatafida (may be written *Laurencia pinnatifida*	Pepper Dulse	Open rocks, middle and lower shore	UK wide

THE GREENS

Latin Name	Common Name	Where it is found	GB Distribution
Ulva intestinalis	Gutweed Sea Grass Hollow Green Seaweed Green Mermaid's Hair Hulk Hair	All shores, tolerates low salinity	UK wide
Ulva lactuca	Sea Lettuce Green Nori Green Laver	All shores and subtidal Tolerates low salinity Nuisance, pollutant where freshwater provides abundant nutirents	UK wide
Ulva linza	Double Ribbon Weed	Midshore and subtidal, often epithetic pollutant (as above)	UK wide
Codium fragile *Codium tomentosum*	Green Sponge Fingers Velvet Horn Dead Man's Fingers	From midshore to low spring tide, often hanging from rocks in rock pools	Scilly Isles Channel Isles South coast, East & West Scotland

Tables by Dr Olivia Bird

Latin Name	Common Name	Where it is found	GB Distribution
The Wracks *Pevetia caniculata*	Channeled Wrack Cow Tang	Upper shore, very sheltered it can survive out of water for days (desiccation)	UK wide
The Wracks *Ascophylum nodosum*	Egg Wrack, Asco, Knotted Wrack, Sea Whistle, Rock Weed, Yellow Tang, Yellow Weed, Norwegian Kelp	Sheltered middle (mostly), doesn't tolerate wave action.	UK wide
The Wracks *Fucus vesiculosus*	Bladder Wrack Rock Weed Popweed, Pigweed Dyer's Focus Kelpware Button Seaweed	Middle shore, lower shore, sheltered rocky. Reasonably tolerant of exposed coast	UK wide
The Wracks *Fucus serratus*	Serrated Wrack Toothed Wrack Saw Wrack	Lower shore, on sheltered or semi-exposed shores	UK wide
Himanthalia elongata	Thong Weed Sea Spaghetti Sea Haricots Spaghetti de Mer Buttonweed	Lower shore, on rocks	UK, except S & SE
Halidrys siliquosa	Sea Oak Pod Weed	Shallow subtidal, and rock pools on lower shore	General UK
Sargassum muticum	Wireweed Japweed	Shallow subtidal and rock pools	Coast S Wales, Ireland, parts of Scotland, invasive
The Kelps *Saccharina Latissima* (formerly *Laminaria saccharina*)	Sugar Kelp, Sea Belt, Poor Man's Weather Glass (or Vane), Sea Tangle, Sweet Kombu, Sugar Wrack	Annual species, prefers less exposed coasts	General UK distribution
Alariaceae vs Laminariaceae Alaria esculenta	Dabberlocks, Honeyware, Badderlocks, Murlins Atlantic Wakame, Wing Kelp, Henware	Subtidal, exposed	Exposed northern & western coasts
The Kelps *Sacchoriza polyschides*	Furbellows	Subtidal, occasionally exposed at very low spring tides	UK, except SE & S coast in general
The Kelps *Laminaria digitata*	Tangle, Oarweed, Sea Girdle, Kombu	Lower shore, subtidal rock pools	General UK, but not SE coast
Laminaria hyperborea	Forest Kelp, Cuvie May Weed, Sea Rods	Subtidal, lower shore	General UK, but not SE coast

Table by Dr Olivia Bird

seaweed will not be heat stressed and will keep fresh for longer. Forage frugally, taking no more than you need, but remember that half a carrier bag of fresh seaweed will reduce to a large jam jar when dried. The good news is that flavour is concentrated as seaweed dries, so less becomes more. There is a traditional Gaelic rhyme that chants the season when each of four seaweeds is best eaten. Translated, it suggests carrageen in spring, dulse in summer, dabberlocks in autumn, and tangle (kelp) in winter, but most folklore focuses on spring. On the Isle of Lewis, the Celtic sea god Shony was treated to ale on Maundy Thursday. Although this religious offering may have tangled Paganism with Christianity, it is interesting that the offering took place in spring. The question of seasonal changes in the nutrient levels of seaweed is frequently raised.

SEASONAL VARIATION

Studies have shown that the chemistry of seaweed changes over the seasons, and future research has the potential to show when a species is more nutrient dense. This would be very useful to the seaweed cook. Literature with regard to when it is best to pick seaweed for home use is sparse. Professor Mike Guiry of NUI Galway tells me that Irish harvesters prefer to pick carrageen after the September spring tides, which concurs with a 1986 paper by Professor Thierry Chopin of the University of New Brunswick. This questions the tradition that St Patrick's Day, in March is the prime time to pick carrageen. Some seaweed toughens over the winter months and other species, such as wireweed, simply disappear as autumn sets in. Having read that pepper dulse picked in late autumn is without flavour, I was surprised to find piquancy in a November harvest – for the casual seaweed collector, some trial and error must be involved. To state the obvious: if a seaweed species is out of season, it won't be available to pick.

Saccharina latissima (Sugar Kelp)

CHAPTER TWO

MOVING INTO THE KITCHEN

THE TASTE OF THE SEA

Sweet, bitter, salty and sour are the four human taste qualities, but relatively recently a fifth, umami, has been added. In 1907 Dr Kikunae Ikeda, a professor of chemistry at the Imperial University of Tokyo, reasoned that there was an element in broth (*dashi*) that made it delicious. He took the liquid used to simmer 38 kg of dried kelp, and succeeded in extracting 30 g of monosodium glutamate (glutamic acid), the real identity of umami. It, umami, is found to a lesser degree in tomatoes, cheese and some sea-foods, but this was a significant moment in food research. On 24 April 1908, Ikeda applied for a patent for his manufacturing method for seasoning with glutamic acid as the key component, and it was registered on 25 July 1908. Ikeda's product, monosodium glutamate (MSG), was quickly patented in the United States, England, and France. Ikeda then took the powdered substance to iodine manufacturer Suzuki Saburō, where in 1909 it was marketed under the brand name Ajinomoto, meaning essence of taste. Newspaper columns began to include Ajinomoto in recipes. However, chefs in Tokyo's restaurants were reluctant to use it because artisan pride compelled them to reject a seasoning that an amateur could make using *dashi*. It was the misfortune of Chinese cooks to be caught overusing MSG in the 1970s and 1980s. Ikeda's finding was made with the aid of a single technician rather than an army of postgraduates, and it was published in Japanese, which meant that not many of the scientific community were able to read it. Another possible hindrance is that the umami taste is mild, almost tasteless even at high concentrations. However, there has been a recent revival of interest in the fifth taste, which bodes well for seaweed. Professor Ole Mouritsen, writing in *Flavour Journal*, recommends the seaweed dulse as a good candidate for umami flavouring, and suggests that flavour can be optimized using a *sous vide*.

Research shows that seaweed has over twice the mineral content of terrestrial plants such as broccoli, tomato or salad, and if used as a taste enhancer is rich in potassium and poor in sodium. The white powdery substance, mannitol, that often covers seaweed is used as a sweetener in the food industry and is medically used as an osmotic diuretic. Mannitol content is five times higher in the kelps than the fucales (fucoids) family of seaweeds and is distinctly visible on sugar kelp and dulse. As a cook, I think of mannitol as ocean-gifted manna, and am happy to leave the medics to its other uses.

Each species of seaweed has its own individual flavour. Some seaweeds bully, others soften when baked, and some, such as dulse, remain chewy when dried. Other seaweeds are kitchen chameleons and change flavour and colour when cooked. A packet or recipe simply labelled seaweed is definitely confusing. Seaweeds deserve better creative descriptions than the wow-word umami. This may happen when British cooks become familiar with using different species of seaweed in the home kitchen.

HARVESTING SEAWEED

Collecting seaweed at low tide could not be described as a fast food experience. The tide must be out, which means that a leisurely stroll is involved. It takes a minimum of twenty-five minutes to walk to one of my favourite seaweed haunts. Accompanied by young children it will take longer. Double this because you must walk back, and you will have spent fifty minutes – and that's without allocating time for gathering seaweed. No time-wasting has been factored in and this presumes that the clock was started on the seashore. Many people pass their time on computers or watching television and I mention the hours that I spend gathering seaweed without resentment. It is an enjoyable pastime but one which is time consuming and, unlike watching television, must coincide with low tide.

Foragers cooking with fresh seaweed must learn the life cycle for each species. At its most tender it will require little cooking, but cooking time must be adjusted for older fronds. It's the same for terrestrial vegetables. Consider young versus older spinach and its different seasonal preparation and cooking time.

After you have collected your seaweed (I will tell you more about the more common edible species later), you will probably need to sit down with a cup of tea. If you have been picking in the colder months, you may need a shower and to warm yourself. In summer, feet will need some attention or you'll redistribute a fine layer of sand throughout your home or seaside rental. Once

Himanthalia elongata and Osmundea pinnatifida.

you are cosy, it is a good idea to sort through your seaweed and coastal plants as soon as possible.

WASHING SEAWEED

The Revd John M'Murtrie wrote: 'Put your seaweeds in a basin of cold fresh water, and all the molluscs instantly let go and fall to the bottom.' Alas, this rarely happens when I wash seaweed. Some people suggest washing seaweed in rainwater before drying it, but I confess that this only happens when I'm forgetful and leave a basket of seaweed on the doorstep. There is a school (to which I don't belong) that rinses and cooks seaweed in seawater. Returning to washing the gathered seaweed – a large sink or at the very least a clear sink and draining board is helpful. If you have managed to put each species of seaweed (or wild plants) into separate bags or containers as I suggest, it will be less of a chore. The shellfish hunters heap their bounty into plastic boxes with tiny holes. These boxes fit snugly into a kitchen sink in colander style, as do some of the garishly coloured plastic baskets that serve as desk tidies. A large colander or sieve will suffice in the absence of shellfish boxes. Rinsing the seaweed in cold water is then relatively easy. It's a question of rummaging through the seaweed and dislodging any stray molluscs, barnacles and isopods. Isopods are very tiny marine crustaceans often no bigger than an ant. Usually they are only visible to the naked eye when the seaweed has been dried. I find lots of isopods after drying pepper dulse. I am sure that I have eaten one or two but I have survived to tell the tale.

EFFECTS OF WASHING ON THE NUTRITIONAL VALUE OF EDIBLE SEAWEED

A Norwegian study (Pierrick Stévant et al, Møreforsking, Norway) into the effects of washing seaweed prepared for human food looked at the adverse effects of removing nutritional water-soluble compounds, and the positive effects of washing-off or reducing anti-nutritional substances and potential toxins. It compared the influence of soaking dabberlocks (*Alaria esculenta*) and sugar kelp (*Saccharina latissima*) in fresh water versus seawater (at different temperatures) to reduce the iodine content. In the case of *S. latissima* hot, fresh water treatments affected iodine, as well as pigment content and colour. In the case of *A. esculenta* only high salinity water (brine) reduced cadmium. This would suggest that prolonged cooking of sea vegetables in hot water (in common with terrestrial vegetables) removes some of the nutritional benefits (minerals and antioxidants).

To preserve taste and avoid possible nutrient loss do not leave fresh seaweed soaking in water. However, soaking will reduce favour so if you are going for a milder taste, soak away. The Victorian author, Margaret Gatty writes in *British Sea-Weeds* (Volume I):

> *There are some plants* [i.e seaweeds] *which will not bear even the touch of fresh water, and which, therefore, must be laid out, as well as cleaned and prepared, in that from the sea. Polysiphonia Brodecei* [sic] *for instance, begins to decompose at once in fresh water… The Griffithsias are nearly as bad. What they do is to crack and let out all their fine pink colouring-matter…*

Mrs Gatty wrote with regard to pressing seaweed, but the advice is relevant. She also notes that if a dozen plants were plunged in the same receptacle some would perish and others would discolour. Conversely, she says that some seaweeds improve by being steeped in water from the well. Rather charitably she writes that collectors would do well to experiment, and if plants are lost by a few mistakes not to grudge them. I suggest applying this principle to cooking seaweed. However, do wash each species separately.

Water temperature may be a problem and if you have a tendency to suffer with cold hands, wear neoprene gloves as you delve about in the seaweed. Carrageen needs particularly careful attention (as does pepper dulse) when it is washed. You will be fortunate if you don't find at least half a dozen tiny snails in a sink full of this seaweed. Remove any discoloured or ragged fronds. If you have a salad spinner this is useful for removing excess water from seaweed fronds. You will now have well washed seaweed in an assortment of colourful piles.

What should you do next? You have various options. You can store the seaweed in a fridge for a couple of days (but no longer), before dealing with it further. In Japan, there has been a revival of harvesting salt based on the ancient methods of the 'amabito', or sea people. Traditionally the *hon'dawara* seaweed was burnt and its ashes mixed with seawater, which was then boiled in small clay pots to produce moshio salt. For the home cook, simmering your preferred seaweed in seawater and then drying the crystals in a large, shallow pan will have the same effect.

You may decide to flash freeze and then bag selected freezer-happy species, or dry the seaweed and watch the volume decrease but the flavour intensify. The choice is yours.

Freezing Seaweed

The temperature of the sea is less liable to variation than that of the air and some seaweeds are confined to temperate or cold climates, others to warmer regions – geography and climate effect distribution. Research papers have been written about the effect of ice on seaweed with regard to climate change, but I could glean little, apart from the fact that knotted wrack would appear to recover relatively well if it becomes covered in snow. It is common sense that freezing tolerance correlates with seaweed zone location, that is to say, the upper shore seaweeds will be more tolerant of the freezer than those found on the lower shore. From personal experience, I am more than happy to cook with dulse that has been frozen. Although I can offer no evidence with regard to its nutrient loss, I can say that it retains its flavour. Dulse defrosts extremely quickly and doesn't freeze as solidly as laver. Laver freezes as hard as the rock to which it was once attached. A 2011 paper looked at the freezing tolerance of nori (laver), which resulted from heavy sea ice forming in the Northern Yellow Sea, China. The results concur with my home freezer experiment: nori has high freezing tolerance and recovers rapidly. I do not freeze the thicker kelps because they contain too much water. They dry exceedingly well. The green seaweed, velvet horn, doesn't freeze; it becomes soggy and spongy. As a rule I don't freeze kelp and rarely freeze the wracks, not least because I don't have to await a spring tide to replenish my wrack stock. I freeze sea spaghetti, but it is best blanched before freezing to avoid a frozen, tangled mass. I flash freeze well-washed dulse in small piles and once frozen, bag it. Laver can be cooked (laverbread) and then flash frozen in small heaps (1–2 tbsps) before bagging and sealing. The green *Ulva spp* freeze well, but I tend to use them fresh or dry.

Dried Seaweed

Drying is one of the oldest methods of food preservation. It involves the removal of moisture to prevent food decay and spoilage. It's important to do this as quickly as possible without actually 'cooking' the food. If the initial temperature is too low, microorganisms may survive. If the temperature is too high and humidity too low, the surface of the seaweed (or coastal ingredient) will toughen but retain inner moisture – a conundrum. Success is a fine balance but comes with practice. If you've picked seaweed in the summer, seaweed can be dried in two days of sunshine. Most seaweed that is on sale in shops or from the internet will be dried. I have listed a directory of dried seaweed suppliers. Some sell fresh seaweed and it may also be available from commercial foragers. Where the seaweed on sale is imported, request it by its appropriate Japanese name: kelp –

kombu, laver – *nori*, sugar kelp/dabberlocks – *wakame*, wireweed – *hjikki*. They are interchangeable for recipes but are not the same species. *Nori* is a quite different species to the laver that we gather on British beaches. Commercially produced seaweed is dried by various methods and many artisan purveyors hand collect their product at low tide. The more caring will, like the amateur seaweed picker, wash the seaweed in the sea to remove sand and any small creatures.

Commercial preserving begins immediately and an amateur should aim not to lag too far behind. Commercial seaweed, where climate permits, is sun-dried by spreading it on nets or over coconut leaves. Artisan purveyors of seaweed often have idiosyncratic drying methods and may be secretive and reluctant to share them. This is a trait they have in common with many foragers of wild food.

The washed seaweed must then be cut into manageable lengths suitable for storage. As the seaweed dries it will shrink considerably. Dried food takes up less space, which is useful for those who live in small apartments. In the home, the simplest way to dry clean seaweed is on newspaper or paper towel lined trays on sunny windowsills, or in a warm airing cupboard. It may also be dried on baking trays in either a low oven (110 °C / Gas ¼), or at speed in a hot oven or under a hot grill. It is ready when it is dry to the touch and crumbles easily. I am wary of the intense heat method because if a cook is distracted, the result will be black and the seaweed will then need to be replenished. I have a similar attitude to toasting pine kernels. The exact time that the seaweed takes to dry is dependent on how much water the seaweed has retained and its thickness. Most seaweed will dry in 2–3 hours in a low oven or food dehydrator. It may also be dry toasted in a shallow, heavy-based pan. On a sunny day without too much wind, larger fronds such as kelp and dabberlocks may be pegged out to dry on a washing line. Scottish tradition says that carrageen is best bleached in the sun on a clover lawn and that it should be rained upon thrice. The clover lawn intrigues me. Had heather or even wild thyme been suggested, I might have been more persuaded.

If the carrageen is rewetted and exposed to the sun, the red and green pigments are bleached, leaving the moss a yellow or straw colour. Some of this bleaching occurs during the initial drying, so that black carrageen always contains a considerable quantity of bleached fronds. For complete bleaching, occasional turning of the moss is required to expose all surfaces to the sun – foreign weeds and other contaminants do not bleach and are easily distinguished in sorting operations while the moss is spread out. My unbleached fronds produce an adequate set.

When drying seaweed, place the fronds so that they do not touch and are uniform in size and thickness. If you dry lots of seaweed, the running costs of a dehydrator will be lower and the drying will be more evenly spread. I use a food dehydrator at a higher and then lower temperature but for best results follow the manufacturer's instructions. Some manufacturers suggest rotating the shelves during drying, if the heat is from the base rather than a fan mechanism. This is also a good idea, if you are drying seaweed in a conventional oven. The simmering oven of a range cooker is often an ideal temperature for drying seaweed. Laid on newspaper, most species of seaweed will dry overnight on the warming area of a range cooker or in a warm airing cupboard.

A novel drying processing method (microwave assisted freeze drying) was tested by the School of Food and Agriculture, University of Maine, United States. It compared the traditional method of oven drying for various colour, moisture content and water activity of dried sugar kelp. Samples oven dried for four hours had on average 10% more moisture than samples using microwave assisted freeze-drying. It was observed that the addition of short-term microwave usage on seaweed samples increases the drying potential without inhibiting product quality. I have yet to experiment. Drying carrageen reduces the moisture

Kelp being harvested on the Isle of Lewis

content from about 85 % to approximately 20 % and the weight to approximately one-fifth of the original. Once dried, seaweed may then be finely ground into a powder in a grinder or by hand with a pestle and mortar, and stored in a tightly sealed, airtight container. One word of advice, grind small quantities at a time if using a liquidiser or electric grinder. Packing a machine full to the gunnels is a recipe for disaster. Ensure the seaweed doesn't heat as you grind because the result will be a sticky mess. Short, sharp bursts on the pulse button is the recipe for success. It can also be stored as is, or broken into smaller pieces and then stored. Dried seaweed is expensive and is often sold in small packs weighing less than 50 g. Frugal recipe followers may consider it prudent to invest in some digital scales. If you have harvested and dried your own seaweed, additional grams may be added 'to taste' without financial worry. Bag seaweed when it is dry.

As Mrs Gatty wrote: 'Whenever it is possible sea-weeds should be laid out on paper and put under pressure the same day they are gathered.' This is interesting, not least because Eydís Mary Jónsdóttir tells me that in Iceland, sol (dulse) is dried first and then weighted.

Storage

Once dried, seaweed may be stored in airtight containers in a cool, dark cupboard or larder for many months. It is a good idea to shake home-dried seaweed periodically and to check the seaweed after a day or two, to ensure that it isn't damp. Storage in clear jars serves as a reminder to not only use the seaweed, but to jiggle it around once in a while. If moisture has dampened seaweed, simply dry it in a low oven or spread it on a tray and leave it in a dry place for a day or two and then re-bag. I tend to keep some dried fronds in 2–3 cm lengths for rehydrating, rather than finely grinding everything. Finely ground dried seaweed however, is extremely useful for seasoning. A 2011 study found that when the farmed, red seaweed Eucheuma was powdered and added to spices, the nutritional quality of the spice was enhanced. I sprinkle ground seaweed into Christmas mincemeat and cake recipes, in the hope that this may have a similar result.

Rehydrating and Cutting Dried Seaweed

Ground, dried seaweed is versatile and easy to use, and an electric grinder or blender ensures finely powdered seaweed. Either is useful for chopping fresh seaweed, although scissors work well too. Cutting larger fronds of dried kelp isn't always easy. Use a sharp knife or scissors and if you need a precise size, soak the seaweed in minimal water first.

Dried seaweed, unless finely ground or in small enough lengths to be added to a casserole etcetera, needs to be rehydrated. Raw seaweed may be fresh or rehydrated. This assumption is made in the recipes. Shop dried seaweed has often been well washed in fresh water (the reason being if the salt content remains high it will be affected by damp – a note for foragers), so its salt content may be lower than that of foraged seaweed. If it is added to recipes in its dried state, liquid levels must be adjusted accordingly. Seaweed expands as it soaks up water and is much easier to cut.

Pre-soaking dried seaweed before use may tenderize it, but some nutrients will be lost. It may be rehydrated in any liquid e.g. in milk, wine or, for flavoured puddings, try diluted wild syrups. The excess soaking water may be used in stock or soup. As a rule of thumb the longer dried seaweed is soaked, the less intense the flavour when eaten. Seaweed may also be rehydrated in a steamer: line the steamer with parchment paper to avoid the seaweed sticking. Heavier dried seaweeds, such as kelps and dulse, can be softened in a marinade including vinegar or lemon juice. Other liquids and sweeteners such as tamari, ginger and honey are useful in marinades too.

Smoked seaweed is now available in shops and seaweed may be home smoked if you have a smoker. I have experimented smoking seaweed over flavoured wood chips but the result was somewhat confused. Historically, the by-product from burning kelp for industrial use was used as a salt substitute by crofters unable to afford salt.

All Change – Colours

Like plants, all seaweeds contain chlorophyll. **Green seaweeds** are green because the pigment chlorophyll is unmodified by other pigments. Their phylum, *Chlorophyta,* is aptly named.

Red seaweeds contain other pigments notably phycobiliproteins. The two main types are phycoerythrin (red) and phycocyanin (blue). The combination of the two conceals chlorophyll, but results in a wide spectrum of colours from deep red to electric blue. The greater the depth, the brighter the colours of seaweed. There are, with the exception of laver, few red seaweeds in the intertidal zone.

Brown seaweeds take their colour from pigments called carotenoids. Among them, fucoxanthin, which absorbs light, is the most common.

The accessory pigments in red and brown seaweeds hide chlorophyll in such a way that the green colour is effectively masked. However, if red or brown seaweed is heated the accessory pigments are denatured and the colour of chlorophyll re-emerges. This is the science behind what appears in the kitchen to be culinary magic.

Dabberlocks changes from brown to olive green when dried or cooked. The mid-rib remains chewy after drying, and for this reason I soak it longer than dried kelp.

Kelp is brown and turns green when cooked and olive green when dried.

Laver becomes a rather unappetizing khaki green when it has been cooked, but tastes delicious.

The wracks, which range in colour from dull olive brown to various greens, will become green when thrown into boiling water. As does brown sea spaghetti.

The *Ulva spp* buck the trend and remain vibrant green when dried or cooked. Carrageen is one seaweed which I usually use in its dried form simply because if you cook with fresh carrageen, you'll need 'shed loads'. It dries to one-fifth of its original volume. After many cookery trials, I now use a carrageen gel in most of my recipes. I've learnt to estimate the amount needed for the required set from the consistency of the gel. The setting agent extracted from seaweed varies very much both in quantity and kind in different genera, and indeed in the case of carrageen varies: in some it as limpid as water, in others like cartilage.

My guess is that it depends when the carrageen has been picked and the exact species. The vigour with which the gel from the carrageen is pushed through the sieve (on a waste not basis) will also determine the quality of the set. Home dried carrageen, dulse and pepper dulse sometimes dry with a white 'calcified' substance. When I first cooked with carrageen I labelled it as a bully, but I've since decided that I was an errant cleaner of the weed. Carrageen is bland, but if it isn't properly prepared it may harbour the scent of other seaweeds or organisms. Milk or cream aids the setting ability of carrageen, so less is required.

Carrageen gel

HOW TO MAKE A CARRAGEEN GEL

Ingredients:

25 g rehydrated carrageen

500 ml water (to cover)

Heat the water and carrageen and simmer over a low heat for 20–25 minutes until the carrageen is thick and gloop like. Strain the carrageen through a fine sieve, pushing as much of the gel through as possible. You should have 3–4 tablespoons of thick gel, which will usually firmly set 300 ml. Professor Mike Guiry suggests that although it may be more difficult to extract the gel from grape pip weed its set is firmer. I usually give the used carrageen fronds a second outing, repeating the process for an extra tablespoon or two of carrageen gel. Alternatively you may use the leftovers to make a handwash.

COOKING AND IODINE CONTENT

Research in Japanese diets has shown that when kelp is boiled for *dashi* it can lose up to 99 % of its iodine content, whilst iodine in wireweed loses only 40 %. However, the variation in iodine content between species and the difficulty in weight terminology (i.e. between dried and fresh seaweeds), may lead to inaccuracy in the suggested iodine content. A 2011 study by Theodore and David Zava suggests that *kombu* (kelp) has the highest iodine content, but they noted that 97 % of dietary iodine is excreted in urine. I will simply note that in Japan, where seaweed is eaten as a part of everyday diet, life expectancy is five years longer than in the USA.

HOMEMADE LAVER

Crafting nori sheets is an arduous task. I suspect that one day somebody will open an English-speaking nori making class, to rival those held in the Omori Nori Museum in Tokyo. I have tried and failed to make a Scottish version of nori.

SEAWEED IS VERSATILE

Many of the seaweeds used in the recipes that follow (see pages 154-231) are interchangeable, but some have a stronger flavour, pepper dulse, for example, which is often used as a condiment. Somewhat bizarrely, I find that seaweed mellows when cooked, particularly after baking. Some species are unpalatable before cooking due to their rubbery texture.

Drying, or the right cooking method, can overcome this. There aren't any hard rules. I tend to cook with seaweed as the Gaels used them in herbal medicine, one at a time. Nature does however blend seaweed naturally as 'mats' or epiphytes. Sometimes I add more seaweed than at others, in much the same way that you add more or less chilli or curry spices. My small jars of dried seaweed are filed in an orderly, colourful fashion in my pantry, and I use them as I would herbs and spices. I usually have some well-washed seaweed fronds in the refrigerator too. Dulse is my stalwart freezer and fridge ingredient. I was interested to read that one author classed sea lettuce as tasting mild. To my palate it veers towards the bully camp.

Writing subjectively, I find that when the kelps, wracks and laver are dried the flavour is subtler than the *Ulva spp*. Seaweed has a huge range of possibilities in the hands of an imaginative cook. If kelp or sea spaghetti is added to a pan of boiling water, culinary magic occurs; it turns emerald green. A small sugar kelp frond will add a caramel glow, as well as subtle flavour, to boiled rice. If seaweed is used to flavour and then pair with vegetables, adjust the cooking times accordingly. Oarweed and forest kelp require long cooking to tenderize, even when finely sliced. Shredded sugar kelp shares even cooking time with root vegetables. Dabberlocks has a tough mid-rib, which demands careful culinary attention. However, when the tougher kelps are dried, ground and sprinkled, you have an instant tenderizer and flavour enhancer.

Seaweed flavoured crisps are available commercially but are

Dr Philip Kerrison from the Scottish Association of Marine Science farming Honeyware or Dabberlocks (Alaria esculenta) on Kerrera Farm, Oban, Argyll

simple to make. Scatter your preferred dried and finely ground seaweed on a baking tray and mix it with minimal oil. Toss thin potato slices into the seaweed mix, and then oven bake until crisp. Seaweed simmered in water makes wonderful stock and in addition to the stock, the cooked seaweed can be eaten as a sea vegetable. Sea lettuce and sugar kelp are perfect for wrapping and cooking papillote. Empty condiment pots can be filled with dried and coarsely ground seaweed, and are ready to shake or even gift away. For a salt fix, mix dried seaweed with home-dried sea salt. The combination competes with those on sale in a food hall and the added value is that it is free. Steaming and poaching are quick and healthy ways to cook and the addition of seaweed adds non-fattening flavour too. Seaweed-infused chicken or fish works particularly well. Our family favourite is scallops sprinkled with dried sea lettuce as they steam. With a little practice cooking with seaweed becomes a part of coastal living.

Palmaria palmata (Dulse)

CHAPTER THREE

SEAWEEDS AND WILD COASTAL EDIBLES

GRAPE PIP WEED

Chondrus crispus & Mastocarpus stellatus

This is a useful seaweed if you are entertaining vegans and are in need of a setting agent. Indeed, carrageen has far more to offer a cook than the blancmange style pudding with which it's traditionally associated. It will also add lustre to sauces or meaty stews that are much appreciated by carnivores. Both its spelling and identification however, are confusing. Indeed it was only out of politeness that I first extracted a gel from grape pip weed. Well aware that my gift wasn't *Chondrus crispus*, I deferred to an Islander's experience and indeed, my panna cotta obtained its set with carrageen, but not the species with which I was more familiar. Dr Alan Imeson, a food scientist suggested that I use the spelling Carrageenan, as one of the terms used in EU regulation (the other being E407), but as this is a book for the home, not the industrial, cook, my preference is for carrageen. It was first called carrageen around 1829. Carrigan Head in Northwest Ireland's County Donegal is thought to be the name's source. Carrageen has, with dulse, been harvested prolifically in the Canadian Province, Prince Edward Island, where it is referred to as 'Irish moss'. However, Canadian recipes passed down from émigré Scots may refer to it in the Gaelic *an cairgein*. Occasionally it is written with an additional 'h' carragheen. Whilst, rather poetically, carrageen is known as *màthair-an-duilisg*, 'the mother of the dulse', which links it with the seaweed dulse. Vernacular names for carrageen are numerous and most countries where it is used in cooking appear to have a local name. In 1844 the American Schmidt extracted carrageenan from *Chondrus crispus,* but the term carrageen now generally refers to the extract obtained from both *Chondrus crispus* and grape pip weed. These two species either individually or together are known as carrageen.

Carrageen picked on British shores might be described as capricious. Its colour varies from purple, red and brown, to white when sun bleached, and it may be relatively smooth or coarse and wiry, not unlike a brillo pad. Grape pip weed is certainly sharp and bristly, when dried. I've carelessly cut myself on dried carrageen but it can also be smooth and iridescent. This isn't the most helpful advice but it's an easy species of British seaweed to gather and its setting properties are useful to a cook. Carrageen is vegan friendly and may be served at warmer temperatures than gelatine. *Chondrus crispus* has flat, wide, fan shaped fronds that branch dichotomously, resembling a mini branching crab apple tree. It would not be out of place in a miniature seaweed garden. Both *Chondrus crispus* and grape pip weed grow on a variety of surfaces on the lower shore, and sub-tidal down to 24 m. The sub-tidal plants are taller and thicker, so it's worth putting on a wetsuit to gather them. Plants further up the shore are easy to access but they are tricky to pick because the frond and stipes are thinner. From the cook's point of view it doesn't matter which species is picked. One recommended practice when harvesting carrageen is to cut the bushy top of the frond, thereby ensuring that the base and holdfast are left intact. Carrageen needs careful washing: rinsing it in seawater before bringing it home is useful and will also re-home some of the many snails that find shelter in it. Carrageen needs as many washes as you can find time to do, and then you need to dry it well. You will need about three times as much fresh as dried carrageen to obtain the same set. When carrageen is dried the quantity needed for a decent set is more manageable. Before use, rinse the carrageen and then soak it in water for 10-15 minutes to rehydrate. Best setting results occur when milk is part of the cooking process. The food scientist Dr Alan Imeson says that when carrageen is used with milk, a specific interaction between kappa carrageenan and kappa casein takes place. Imeson says that in general, 0.3 % carrageen mixed with milk, gives the same gel strength as 0.8 – 1.0 % in water. So, succinctly, if milk is involved in your culinary creation, less carrageen is needed. I may not be a chemist but I do add a teaspoon of carrageen gel to soften homemade ice-cream.

An interesting but little know fact about carrageen is that along with rosehips it was foraged for the Second World War effort. After Pearl Harbour, when the Japanese supply was cut off, the Ministry of Health was concerned about the supply of agar for medicinal and food purposes. Professor Lily Newton, who was a member of the Vegetable Drugs Committee of the Ministries of Supply and Health, foraged with colleagues and students for various carrageens as a substitute for Japanese agar.

Without this work the deficit of agar would have had a far more serious effect on bacteriology supplies for Public Health, for the production of penicillin, and for the preparation of vaccines, both for the civilian population and for the military. As Newton (1951: 129) stated: 'When it is realised that over 240 tons of carrageen were collected round the shores of Britain in three years, from plants which are only a few inches long, some idea is obtained of the effort involved.' The most important service that agar renders to mankind in war or peacetime is as a bacteriological culture medium. After the war the production of carrageenan extraction expanded significantly. The war propelled carrageenan into a major role in food production and is the reason that it continues to be the main seaweed extract used worldwide.

N.B. With the exception of Japanese nori, the production of seaweed hydrocolloids consumes the largest amount of macro algae annually, and carrageenan is the largest consumer of this group. However, there is controversy (amongst academic researchers) surrounding carrageenan which suggests that in a human diet it may contribute to chronic inflammation. This relates to industrially-processed carrageenan, which is extracted from various red seaweeds, mainly Eucheumas. It has nothing to do with the setting agent obtained from *Chondrus crispus* or *Mastocarpus stellatus* i.e. the carrageen used in old fashioned (and contemporary!) kitchen recipes.

DULSE
Palmaria palmata

Dulse has many colloquial names: *dillisk* is Irish, *duiliasg* is Gaelic. Dulse should not be confused with red rags (*Dilsea carnosa*). Dulse (*Palmaria palmata*) is thinner and more slippery. There is confusion because red rags is often called false dulse. Dulse is also called: creathnach, water leaf, sheep's weed, handed fucus, red kale and, in Iceland, sol. It is one of my

Dilsea carnosa, **False Dulse or Red Rags and two species of** *Fucus.* **The yellow-brown one is** *Fucus vesiculosus* **and the darker brown one below is** *Fucus serratus*

favourite seaweeds not least because its history is European. Dulse cooks quickly and the umami fix reminds me of bacon. A cheap supper recipe is a simple dulse and potato cake. The naturalist author Euell Gibbons suggests that its flavour is only appreciated by long chewing. Perhaps those who loathe dulse don't masticate long enough to become enthusiastic. Gibbons described eating fresh dulse thus: 'It was tough and elastic, and the sensation was like chewing on a salted rubber band. However, when I hung some of it on a wire under my porch roof and dried it for a week, it entirely changed, both in taste and texture.' Unlike some dried seaweeds, dulse doesn't become overly brittle. It remains pliable, which is why it makes good gum. Dulse was eaten raw by coastal workers to ward off hunger, but it is much more palatable when cooked. F. Marian McNeill writes in *The Scots Kitchen* (1929) that: 'Dulse is said to be in perfection when it has three times bathed in the May flood', and traditional folklore suggests that spring and early summer are the best times to pick dulse. To be candid, I have noticed little seasonal variance in taste.

DULSE KNOW HOW

Dulse is ruby red in colour with an occasional purple hue. Older specimens may be leathery, brown and ragged. The fan like frond size is variable (it can grow up to 50 cm) and it can be found throughout the UK. The single blade is often divided into what I describe as fingers with rounded tips; others may say it resembles a fork. Dulse grows on sheltered and exposed areas in the inter- and sub-tidal zones. The holdfast is disc like and small, so take care that you don't yank it out and prevent further growth. It grows on rocks and even shellfish, but it is also epiphytic, meaning it grows non parasitically on other seaweeds. The dulse blades divide into what might be called bladelets, which often hang elegantly from a kelp stipe. The red pigment in red seaweeds is water-soluble which means that when soaked and used in cooking, it will naturally shade pink until it is cooked and then it becomes green. When I collect storm-cast dulse, which has hitched a ride on a thin kelp stipe, I often bring the kelp and dulse partnership home. I've tried leaving the dulse attached to the kelp stipe and refrigerating the lot, hoping that it retains freshness in the way that soil on root vegetables is useful. In my experience it makes no difference. Dulse is easy to wash. A couple of rinses in clean water will remove seaside debris and then, it just needs a good shake in a colander. If you have a salad spinner this works very well. Dulse freezes but a lazy cook, who doesn't remove excess water, will find pink crystals surrounding the seaweed when he or she retrieves it from the freezer. The pink ice is soon shaken off. Dried dulse will remain a little malleable, this is why it makes good gum.

LAVER

Porphyra spp

Laver is an accepted food. In China porphyra is called *tsuts'ai,* in Japan *amanori,* and in Wales *bara lawr.* It is also known as purple laver, sloke and black butter in England, *slouk* in

Scotland, or *sleabhac* in Ireland.

In *Good Things in England* (1932), Florence White says: 'According to recent scientific research laver is rich in iodine. If we had had the business acumen of the French we should have made it as famous as truffles of Perigeux.' Indeed the Welsh have a very good laverbread industry. The wild food enthusiast and naturalist author Euell Gibbons writes that laver is tenderer than dulse and can be nibbled raw, but concedes that it's better half dried before being eaten. His assessment that laver is one of the better seaweeds for cooking and makes a pretty fair soup is, however, spot on.

Laver is often muddled into the word laverbread, which is synonymous with a Welsh breakfast. Laver is gathered on the Pembrokeshire and Gower coastline and then canned, so perhaps it is unsurprising that cooked laver is on sale in Welsh supermarkets. However by UK standards local seaweed (albeit cooked) on sale in a supermarket is a rarity. British laver is not *Porphyra yezoensis* or *Porphyra tenera* or nori, as it is known in Japan. Nori has been cultivated on a huge scale, whereas laver is wild and common around the entire British coast. There are various species which experts will be able to differentiate between. The blades are one or two cells thick (it's thin) and its low-density means that if you pick it, ensure that the holdfast is left on the rock to allow future growth.

LAVER KNOW HOW

Porphyra is the Latin for water plant and the Greek word for purple, but laver can be purple, green or almost black. Whatever its colour it is classed as a red seaweed and unlike most of the reds, grows in the intertidal zone. This is good news for the forager because harvesting is not dependent on a low spring tide. It grows on rocks and even pebbles on all levels of sandy beaches. If it's windy, it's incredibly difficult to prise from the rocks. My local laver resembles a thin, crinkled black bin liner. The easiest way to harvest laver is in the rain or as the tide comes in. The fronds float from the rocks with the flow of water and then you must take your chance with scissors, remembering to leave a decent amount with the holdfast. Laver needs a good wash and as many rinsings through a sieve or very fine colander as you can find time for. Laver harbours sand – when you think it's clean, I suggest at least two more washes.

The author Dorothy Hartley notes that: 'real devotees prefer their laver neat and strong'. The Revd David Landsborough says that laver was: 'Boiled for hours, reduced to a pulp and eaten with either lemon juice or butter and spices.' Interestingly he said that it was seldom eaten in Scotland except by the affluent under the name of laver. His own experience didn't rate it, unless it was cooked in butter, verifying the Scottish proverb: 'If you boil *stanes* (Scots for stones) in butter, you may sup the broo.' Butter makes it taste good. Landsborough or indeed the BBC journalist and food writer Derek Cooper, who is also on record as not being a laver fan, may not have been aware of a butter-enriched dish called *Tobhtal*, which was popular on the Isle of Lewis. The recipe is not unlike Welsh laverbread but butter is added to the cooked laver. On the Isle of Barra, *slokan* was made. This involved simmering laver with minimal seawater until it was cooked to a pulp and then butter and seasoning were added. It was served hot with potatoes. I cook laver in minimal water, in a heavy based pan. Cookery books will suggest that it's simmered for hours but 2-3 hours is quite long enough. Drain the cooked laver well and mince it in a blender. It can then be put in a jar and refrigerated for 4-5 days, or frozen. I often sprinkle dried laver on grilled tomatoes for a double umami fix. I also cook raw laver with potatoes and mash them together. The laver retains some texture. We like this, but it isn't nursery food. Dorothy Hartley suggests: 'the iodine flavour is sometimes disliked at first, but few people care for olives or oysters instantly!' I concur and love her comparison of laver to stockings: 'Like thin brown silk clinging to the rocks between tide marks.'

Margaret Gatty, of whom I will talk at length in Chapter Five, often made small books using seaweeds arranged non scientifically and benefiting from plain speaking text to give to friends. In one volume (1873) she mentions *Porphyra lacinia*.

> *This is the laver of the epicure, and is sold in jars in the Italian Warehouses. It is a great delicacy when properly dressed and kept at boiling heat in a silver dish by means of a spirit lamp. It is eaten with a few drops of lemon juice squeezed over it. In ignorant hands and turned out after dressing into a common dish it is almost, if not quite nasty. For it is gelatinous and as soon as it begins to cool, becomes a sticky mess, which neither lemon nor anything else can make palatable.*

It is common in most places. Laver is delicious even if you weren't born with a silver spoon in your mouth. The less affluent people of Gatty's day who resided on the Gower peninsula in Wales would have confirmed this.

An expert might identify seven species in the UK but most of us will just gather it when we can. I'm told that commercial harvesters gather from October to April but I pick laver over the year, as spied, and prepare and cook it in the same way. Like spinach, laver reduces in volume when cooked.

GLASSWORT OR MARSH SAMPHIRE
Salicornia europaea

Glasswort is also known as poor man's asparagus, pickleweed or sea bean, amongst many colloquial names. It grows on salt marshes, often around estuaries, and resembles a plant from *Jurassic Park*: it looks like mini cacti without the prickly spikes. It is packed with alkali, which is why it was used in the manufacture of old English glassware. This is where the name glasswort originated. An old indigenous British plant, it can form lawns when allowed and is steeped in British history. Glasswort has been harvested as an edible by generations of coastal dwellers.

Glasswort or Marsh Samphire

Glassmakers built their huts in amongst the marsh samphire for convenient harvesting. The herbalist Nicholas Culpeper praised the cleansing qualities of the juice of glasswort. In an industrial move from soap, some species of marsh samphire (there are lots and they are difficult to identify) are now cultivated off shore from Saudi Arabia, Eritrea and Mexico for the production of oil. In the winter months these cultivated plants make their way into British shops, as does glasswort from Israel. It's a delicious wild ingredient that British supermarkets are happy to supply to those keen to eat glasswort out of season.

In Britain between June and September glasswort is abundant on many parts of the coastline, Norfolk in particular. Glasswort grazing lamb commands a high price at the butcher's shop. Historically, fishmongers repaid customer loyalty with a sprig or two of glasswort in parcels of fish. Some say that the best plants are washed by the tides, but I'm not sure that I could taste the difference. Age is the key factor – pick high up the stem because the base becomes woody with age. The roots belong to the landowner and must remain. Forage as early in the season as possible. The glasswort season begins on midsummer's day but it is often into the month of July before I spy it in Scotland.

When picking glasswort decent footwear is essential, and you need a pair of scissors and a basket or bag. Kneeling is my preferred option but test the sand/mud for terra firma, otherwise it is a backbreaking business. This is the most delicious wild plant and when young, there is nothing nicer than carefully picking the tips (don't yank up any roots) from the muddy sand, washing it in clean seawater and popping it into an egg or salmon sandwich. It is crunchy and bursts with seaside juices.

If you are lucky, you might spy purple sea asters or sea purslane nearby. These leaves are equally tasty in sandwiches. Glasswort marries well with poached eggs, fish (with a hollandaise, if you aren't on a diet) and lamb. I wash and rinse glasswort several times under running water before using it. Refrigerate pickings in an unwashed state and wash as required. Traditionally both marsh and rock samphire were pickled for preservation. The author Patience Gray suggests that they are interchangeable in recipes. The author Jason Hill, however, concurs with Hartley et al and writes of marsh samphire: 'it makes a wholesome, though rather insipid vegetable dish, but it lacks the characteristic flavour of the true samphire'. He adds: 'It cannot be used as a pickle.' I do pickle glasswort, but my preference for both is fresh is best. Identification of glasswort is relatively easy but if you are anxious, check out a decent fishmonger's counter before you head off to the beach.

Pepper Dulse
Osmundea pinnatifida

Pepper dulse has small, lacy fernlike fronds and a piquant peppery flavour. It is often overlooked and doesn't appear to feature in folklore remedies. This may be because, as Professor Mike Guiry suggests, its flavour comes from molecules called terpenes, which have a protective function and deter grazing molluscs and fish. For this reason he suggests that it is consumed in moderation. I enjoy its flavour, but it is difficult to prise from the rocks and takes time to harvest. The French botanist Camille Sauvageau recorded that its special odour and piquancy is only evident in young plants

Pepper dulse

collected in winter and spring, and that by autumn little is left in older plants. I question this because my autumn gatherings are garlic scented. Although the gatherings were icy affairs and, unlike summer pickings, there was a calcified covering on the dried fronds. The phycologist Amelia Griffith sampled pepper dulse and considered it excellent. This nineteenth century lady was unusual because most Westerners of her era didn't include seaweed in their diet, unless there was a serious food shortage. In 1856 the Dickensian journal *Household Words* reported that the dulse-wives of Aberdeen sold pepper dulse, but it appears to have been mixed with the unrelated dulse (*Palmaria palmata*). Pepper dulse may be lighter to carry but it's more time-consuming to harvest: 'Pepper-dulse – *Laurencia pinnatifida* – is much more rare and more piquant than *Iridea edulis*. At Aberdeen every dulse-wife has ordinarily a few handfuls of pepper-dulse, half-a-dozen plants of which she adds, when asked, to every halfpenny worth of dulse. Sometimes there is one who, being weakly, has nothing but pepper-dulse, which is less heavy to carry, and more costly than the common breakfast relish of the Aberdonians.'

PEPPER DULSE KNOW HOW

Pepper dulse is a red seaweed and varies in colour from red-brown, pale yellow, greenish olive or purple, depending on exposure to the sun and where it has been picked. It varies in form and is similar to royal fern weed (*Osmundea osmunda*), but this is a much larger (and consequentially easier to pick) species growing to 20 cm in length. It is impossible to identify the *Osmundea* species without the base. This is stoloniferous in pinnatifida and discoid in *Osmunda*. Pepper dulse grows to 8 cm and has a tangled creeping hold, which makes it very tricky to pick sustainably without damaging the holdfast. Its frond is thick, almost fleshy with alternate branching, and appears flattened as if it has been pressed. It thrives on open rocks in the middle and lower shores. There is also an epiphytic *Osmundea oederi*, which often attaches itself to the *Fucus* species. This species is confined to the south and west coast of Britain. The other species, pepper dulse (*Osmundea pinnatifida*) is found throughout the UK coast. Pepper dulse takes considerable time to pick. Scissors are really the kindest way to collect this seaweed (to ensure that you don't cut the twisted holdfast) and a mixed bag of small particles of rock and sand seem unavoidable. Scissors don't work very well on gloved hands. In autumn harvesting is hard and cold work. Some say that it tastes of fish, but to my palate there is a distinct taste of garlic. A handful of fresh pepper dulse fronds simmered in 600 ml water makes a wonderful pink, piquant stock, which is excellent for risotto. I usually dry pepper dulse rather than freeze it. I think that this is, in part, due to the time that it takes to harvest. It seems a little indulgent to cook with fresh. Succinctly, this seaweed is hard work to harvest but worth it. For my palate, less is more.

KELPS (INCLUDING DABBERLOCKS)

The kelps are often interchangeable for cooking purposes and would most probably have been for folklore medicinal purposes. The discovery of umami surrounded the use of *kombu* (kelp) in Japanese *dashi*. It responds to 'slow' cooking for stock making. Kelp is rich in natural glutamate as well as being a good source of iodine. Alginic acid is extracted from kelp and is used by the food industry for binding, thickening and moulding. Algin accounts for kelp's flexibility and its ability to withstand the surge of the waves.

OARWEED
Laminaria digitata

Oarweed may also be called sea girdles, sea wand, and red ware. Makombu, Ebisume, Habariko-Kombu, Hirome, Minmaya-Kombu, Moto-Kombu, Oki-Kombu, Powdered Kombu, Shinori Kombu, Uchi-Kombu, Umiyama-Kombu are all local names for *Laminaria japonica* or *kombu*, which is not the same species as the kelp that you see on British shores. Some British seaweed harvesters still insist on calling UK-harvested kelp *kombu*. Oarweed grows at low tide level on rocky shores and is found in lower shore rock pools. It is without a mid-rib and the stipe is flexible and smooth. The large brown fronds are leathery and divided into thin straps, which spread out like fingers. It falls prostrate on the shore when the tide is out. Its flexibility allows it to flow with the crashing wave as it batters the coast. The oarweed forest marks the boundary between land and sea, and its fronds provide habitat and grazing to a large variety of molluscs, including the translucent blue-rayed limpet. This small mollusc eats its way into the stipe, therein weakening it and causing storm breakage. When harvesting kelp, don't remove the holdfast, cut well up the stipe, and pick a little here and there. If cooking kelp stipes for consumption rather than stock, do not consider using anything over 1 cm thick.

FOREST KELP
Laminaria hyperborea

Laminaria is from the Latin *lamina*, meaning thin layer, and the Hyperboreans were a legendary people believed to live beyond the north wind in a land of unbroken sunshine. I'm unsure about the sunshine, but it is a northerly growing seaweed. At about a metre below the low water level, forest kelp replaces the oarweed forest. Forest kelp is the most dominant UK kelp but it is never exposed at low tide. Kelp plants occur in cold water up to about 7 m below the low water mark. The depth of any kelp forest is restricted by poor light penetration. In the clearest waters it can extend further, perhaps to 15-20 m. Forest kelp is similar to oarweed but is distinguished by its stiff stipe. It is also characteristically rough, which allows epiphytes (e.g. dulse) to attach and in so doing the epiphytes grab extra light to photosynthesize. The fronds decay and break away from the tip of the stipe in winter, thereby permitting new growth. New fronds grow rapidly in the spring and the old frayed frond is forced away by new growth. Its holdfast is perennial and may be up to fifteen years old or more.

Furbellows
Saccorhiza polyschides

Furbellows is the largest European brown algae. It is more common in sheltered waters, and probably not as obvious to the casual observer as oarweed. The blade is similar to that of oarweed and forest kelp but it is distinguished by its frilly stipe and warty holdfast, which makes me wonder if it has taken its name from furbelow, with its petticoat association.

Sugar Kelp
Saccharina latissima

Sugar kelp may also be called sea belt, poor man's weather vane, sweet kombu, kombu royale or sugar wrack. This is found in relatively sheltered areas (as is furbellows). Its long, wavy frond reminds me of a mermaid's tail. It is mid brown in colour and has a much shorter and thinner stipe than oarweed and forest kelp. Dabberlocks and sugar kelp (both stipe and fronds) are my favourite brown seaweeds to cook with. The weakness of the sugar kelp stipe doesn't mean that it can't grow

Fronds of dabberlocks (with a mid-rib) and sugar kelp

to hand towel width and metres beyond its width in length. When placed in boiling water sugar kelp turns an incredible shade of emerald green. It is stunning and delicious.

GIANT KELP
Ecklonia maxima & Macrocystis pyrifera

There is now only one giant kelp species in Pacific USA, South Africa, Australia and NZ. It can grow at 1 m per day but 60 cm is more typical. The way that kelp affects a surfing experience is different according to location and species. In Scotland, *Laminaria hyperborea* is quite short in length and sits below the water level at mid or high tide, where a mattress of kelp will cushion a surfer's wipe-outs. At low tide, however, it will make walking out to the break treacherous. In Southern Africa, the dominant species of kelp is *Ecklonia maxima*. This grows in extremely dense patches in the surf zone and can make paddling out a comical experience. It is irritating at low tide, because the kelp will stick up in the middle of the wave and can stop a surfer dead in the water. The giant kelp found in California is *Macrocystis pyrifera*, it tends to grow in large forests beyond the surfers' breakpoint. It has been suggested that it doesn't effect surfing Instead, it filters out the short-period chop, resulting in a cleaner, smoother wave at the surfer's line-up.

DABBERLOCKS
Alaria esculenta

It is also known as murlins, honeyware, Atlantic wakame, wing kelp, henware, badderlocks and wild wakame. Latin scholars will feel confident eating this seaweed because *esculenta* translates as edible. Indeed in *A Natural System of Botany* (1836), John Lindley suggested that 'when stripped of the thin part [by which I think he means the mid-rib] the beautiful *Alaria esculenta* forms a part of the simple fare of the poorer classes of Ireland, Scotland, Iceland, Denmark and the Faroe Islands'. Dabberlocks is a brown to olive green seaweed that grows on exposed coasts. This is interesting because it is delicate, and as a consequence older specimens often look battered, frayed and torn at the tip and the sides of the frond. The leathery mid-rib holds the fading frame together. Rachel Carson in *The Edge of the Sea* (1955) writes: 'Its long, ruffled, streaming fronds rise with each surge and fall as the water pours away seaward. The fertile *pinnae*, in which the reproductive cells mature, are borne at the base of the frond, for in a plant so exposed to violent surf this location is safer than the tips of the main blade. Almost more than any seaweed Dabberlocks is conditioned to constant pounding of the waves.' Miss Joy Sandison of Unst (Shetland Isles) recalls that children found its mid-rib crunchy and sweet and ate *hinnie waar* as a sweetie.

DABBERLOCKS KNOW HOW

Its new growth is produced at the base of the frond and can be up to 5 m long. It has the most distinct mid-rib (line downs its middle) and 'wings'. Its holdfast is claw like and stipe thick, which makes excellent *dashi* or stock. If I find storm cast dabberlocks (on a clean beach) with wings intact I am a happy person. I was

Dabberlocks wings

delighted to read that Dawson Turner in his *Historia Fucorum* (1809) concurs: 'This plant is much eaten in Scotland, the parts employed for that purpose are the midrib, stripped of its membrane, which is extremely sweet (as the children on Shetland found) and the thick part of the *pinnae*, which are called keys.' The wings need minimal cooking and, when steamed, are the most delicious sea vegetable. Wings, thinness and the lack of wacky frond embossment will distinguish dabberlocks from sugar kelp. Dabberlocks is always submerged. It is found in the sub-tidal on wave-exposed areas. It could be confused with the invasive Japanese *wakame* (*Undaria pinnatifida*) which has a curvier edge.

COOKING STIPES
Thin kelp stipes really are worth it. I hadn't had much of a chance to cook the new season stipes until recently. Cut into 2 cm pieces and pop in a pressure cooker with minimal water for 20 minutes. Allow the pressure to reduce at room temperature (say 10 minutes). A handful per person is sufficient as a sea vegetable.

COOKING THE KELPS
Sugar kelp, when finely shredded, will cook al dente within 15-20 minutes and even its young stipes cook in 20 minutes in a pressure cooker. I only cut stipes where the seaweed is prolific and even

then, never more than one or two. The sugar kelp stipe is thinner than those of forest kelp and oarweed, but if you are fortunate enough to find thin *Laminaria* stipes these too may be cooked in a pressure cooker and either served as a vegetable, added to a slow casserole or pickled. Kelp species are, unless young, too thick to eat raw or cook quickly. The mid-rib as the children of Unst discovered, is sweet. Dabberlocks is lighter than the kelps and so it dries relatively quickly. I use dried and crumbled kelp as standard seasoning, rather I suspect in the way that the Japanese use kelp in *dashi*. It is versatile and makes an excellent store cupboard base for instant stock. Once dried, kelp is a natural ingredient with a long shelf life and is cheaper than a stock cube too.

ORACHE
Atriplex spp

Orache is the coastal alternative to spinach and its appearance varies by species. It sprawls over the splash zone, above decaying seaweed and on to coastal paths, occasionally growing to some height. The leaves are triangular or spear shaped and vary in colour from dark green to frosty grey, which looks as if it has been lightly dusted with icing sugar. Orache requires little preparation and is a delicious summer food. It can, when young, be eaten raw, quickly boiled spinach-style, or baked in a quiche or savoury muffins. Gather and eat this green whenever you can, its re-growth is speedy and it can be frozen too. It's a very good idea to become acquainted with the versatile coastal oraches.

ROCK SAMPHIRE
Crithmum maritimum

Rock samphire is pronounced *samfire* and glasswort or marsh samphire is pronounced *samfur*. It is also commonly known as sea fennel or St Pierre. The author Colin Spencer writes: 'rock samphire was a food for all, especially the elite. So great was

Rock samphire (*Crithmum maritimum*)

society's addiction to this plant that it vanished entirely and now we have completely forgotten how to search for it'. Rock samphire is native to most parts of coastal Britain but not to northern Scotland. The leaves were traditionally pickled. Herbal medicine claims it is beneficial for digestion. Both the great herbalists, Gerard and Culpeper, write of its medical worthiness. The food writer Dorothy Hartley suggested that 'you can smell rock samphire before you find it. Among all of the unique smells of the country, samphire holds unique place. People who dislike it say it smells of sulphur, others sniff it ecstatically, and seem to make themselves slightly drunk on the aroma. Some say dislike, try again and like. Liking is so uncontrolled, some families from miles away from the sea get it sent to them. Nobody is neutral.'

Interestingly, although she enthused about rock samphire Hartley is rather dismissive of glasswort or marsh samphire, which rock samphire is frequently confused with. Rock samphire is a succulent, seashore plant with bitterness to it. I find its scent milder than creosote, the substance to which those averse to the plant compare it. Its cacti shaped leaves are thin and elongated and have a lemony taste. Eat the leaves whilst young and tender, before the end of May when the plant has small umbels of yellow flowers. In late summer and early autumn, its seeds are useful to the cook too. Rock samphire grows in rock crevices and on sheer cliff faces and was mentioned by Shakespeare in *King Lear.* 'Hangs one that gathers samphire, dreadful trade!' (Act IV, Scene VI.)

On the Isle of Wight a landowner charged an annual rent for the 'privilege' of scaling steep cliffs to harvest rock samphire. This was, as the botanist William Coles wrote in *Adam in Eden, or Nature's Paradise* (1657), a dangerous practice, 'for some have ventured so far upon the craggy precipices that they have fallen down and broken their necks, so that it might be said they *paid* for their sawces'. Coles added, however, that 'of all the sawces (which are very many) there is none so pleasant, none so familiar and agreeable to Man's body as samphire'. Geoffrey Grigson in *The Englishman's Flora* writes that, in May, rock samphire packed in casks filled with seawater was transported to markets in London. It was indeed a prized herb. Some less scrupulous market traders would sneakily put marsh samphire (glasswort) at the bottom of their bundles instead, which was, as Philip Miller wrote in his *Abridgement of the Gardener's Dictionary* (1771), 'a great abuse, because this plant has none of the warm aromatic taste of the true samphire'. Perhaps Miller's view encouraged Dorothy Hartley's poor comparison of marsh to rock samphire.

Samphire Hoe, as mentioned by Shakespeare, derived its name from the cliffs where rock samphire was collected, but sadly rock samphire is no longer in abundant supply in Britain today. It may, as is the case with some seaweed species, have been a victim of Victorian overharvesting. It does not grow in the north of Scotland and yet, where it takes root, its growth is prolific. I found an abundant supply on a coastal path in Cornwall which I gathered and wrapped in dampened newspaper. It survived a journey to the Outer Hebrides and continued to thrive on a window ledge for a fortnight. The seeds of rock samphire may be dried and add aromatic flavour to baking, and may be used as an alternative to capers.

Sea aster (*Aster tripolium*)

SEA ASTER
Aster tripolium

This pretty, mauve flowering coastal plant thrives in salty conditions, where it can carpet large areas of salt marshes and paths. It flowers from late summer through to the autumn, cheering up the shortening summer days. Sea aster, marsh and rock samphire are sea vegetables which have grown in popularity recently. Historically, the rich succulent leaves were eaten in times of famine but today they are considered a delicacy. The leaves are thick to enable them to retain moisture when sprayed with salt from the sea. Tossed in butter and served with fish or lamb, sea aster leaves make a simple but delicious sea vegetable.

SEA-BUCKTHORN
Hippophae rhamnoides

Sea-buckthorn is also known as sea berry. Add a hyphen to differentiate sea-buckthorn from buckthorn, which has many variants, and that done a forager taps his or her seasonal finger waiting for autumn, when the spiny coastal shrub displays its vivid orange berries. The common sea-buckthorn is the most widespread variety. It grows in coastal areas where it can withstand salt sprayed from the sea. Interestingly, county councils plant sea-buckthorn borders as a thorny deterrent to vandals, but birds and foragers are grateful. The berries survive at up to 14,000 ft in Tibet and the Himalayas, where their medical benefit is well documented. The Greeks fed this ancient food to their horses, whose coats were said to have benefitted. Its botanical name *Hippophae* means 'shiny horse'. More recently scientists have acknowledged that it is nutrient dense. It is rich in Vitamins, omega 3, 6, 7 and 9, fatty acids, amino acids, folic acid and flavonoids. It has been suggested that it has more omega oils than any other food source and considerably more Vitamin C than is found in oranges. Its new addition to the 'super food' range is impressive, but it remains an ingredient that is free to coastal foragers. The courteous gatherer will ensure that he or she takes enough for his own cooking pot and no more, leaving plenty for others, including the birds. Bird carriage will encourage the distribution of sea-buckthorn further afield.

SEA-BUCKTHORN KNOW HOW

The berries are embedded in the thorny branches and squish if the harvester's touch is anything but delicate. Harvesting the orange berries is a labour of love. The berries are tart and there's little to encourage a child to pick them. The branches are prickly, the berries fiendishly difficult to pick, and the smell isn't pleasant. However, sea-buckthorn oil contains a natural sun protection and was used after Chernobyl to heal radiation burns. Filling a basket takes time and even a careful gatherer will find silvery green leaves in the basket. The leaves are used in tisanes but I cook with them too. Wear gloves and be prepared to spend time gathering. Ideally choose firm berries that you can then flash freeze and bag and store in the freezer until use. A rogue berry will taint others, so be discerning

Sea-Buckthorn *(Hippophae rhamnoides)*

as you pick. You might also pack the washed and dried sea-buckthorn berries into a small bottle with sugar, vodka or gin for liqueurs, or use them in vinegars or jellies. They are rich in pectin, so mix well with fruits with poor setting power. The extracted juice can be sweetened with honey and diluted with sparkling water as a refreshing drink or used in sorbets – two parts sea-buckthorn juice to one sugar syrup.

SEA OAK
Halidrys siliquosa

Sea oak, also called pod weed, is the colloquial name for two seaweed species, one red and one brown. The brown sea oak is a seaweed with stalked and jointed thin air pods. It is found in rock pools on the middle to lower shore throughout the UK. When it is exposed at very low spring tides, it can carpet vast areas of the shallow sub-tidal. Interestingly, I have seen it growing on what appears to be sand on Hebridean beaches. Younger species are olive green and may be muddled with wireweed but the pods are quite different. It is easily relieved of sand, a quick rinse suffices and it dries quickly. Some seaweed cooks add acid to soften

Sea oak *(Halidrys siliquosa)*

seaweed. Sea oak (and kelps) may on occasion, benefit from the addition of lemon or vinegar.

SEA SPAGHETTI

Himanthalia elongata

Sea spaghetti is also known as sea bean, thong weed, buttonweed, sea haricots or *spaghetti de mer*.

The translation of the Latin name of this seaweed is a helpful clue to its identity; it means elongated or long. It is indeed. It looks like floating pasta. When seen hanging from rocks it can carpet large platforms at low water mark. It is only exposed at the lowest spring tide. However, once you have spied your local crop it is well worth a paddle (or a swim at neap tide) to gather this delicious seaside vegetable. The flat, rope-like fronds may grow to over a metre and stream from a distinct looking button. The spaghetti fronds float with the flow of the tide. Lift the sea spaghetti and around its sticky buttons you may find pepper dulse or carrageen. Young sea spaghetti (harvested in spring and early summer) can be eaten raw or cooked in noodle cooking time. As the season progresses it will take longer to cook al dente,

Sea spaghetti *(Himanthalia elongata)*

and by late summer you will need to remove an outer slippery hairy coat before cooking. The fronds die back in autumn so its season is not dissimilar to terrestrial vegetables. It provides a natural base to pair with traditional pasta accompaniments. For an added twist, cook sea spaghetti 50:50 with wheat pasta. As it cooks the brown seaweed turns green. Sea spaghetti growth is at the frond divide, so bear this in mind when harvesting. If there is plenty, pick a few of the holdfast buttons (receptacles) early in the season. The young buttons are delicious raw in early summer salads. They can also be pickled.

In French shops, where sea spaghetti is hand harvested commercially at low spring tides, you will see jars marked *Haricot de Mer* – this is sea spaghetti. It is suggested by the producers that the jars are drained of the salt water and lemon extract, and used in a salad or stir-fry. These ideas resonate with my thoughts – simple ideas are often best. One company sells sea spaghetti in a *framboise vinaigre*, another culinary option. It is also canned or jarred in Portugal and Spain too. I use this seaweed in place of pasta, and frequently blanche and refresh it for use in salads. It is extremely versatile and cooks quickly. Marinate sea spaghetti as they do in France, or enjoy it Italian style in a carbonara sauce.

SEA BUTTONS (THE HOLDFAST OF SEA SPAGHETTI)

The small button-like frond appears in late winter to early spring. I've spied them as early as January on the Outer Hebridean Isle of South Uist. From these buttons, the long, narrow, strap-like reproductive fronds are formed. Historically, in Scotland the buttons were used in sauces for poultry. Sea spaghetti is also known as button-weed, after its discoid holdfast. The saucer-shaped button has a cartilage-like consistency, but when young it tastes delicious raw – or indeed pickled. The young, dichotomously branched vegetative fronds can also be eaten raw, straight from the rocks too. Young, raw sea spaghetti fronds and buttons are tender and work well in salads and pasta dishes. A word of caution: only forage where the buttons are prolific and don't be greedy.

SEA SPAGHETTI KNOW HOW

Chorda filum also known as Mermaid's Tresses or Bootlace Weed, is similar to sea spaghetti but it is an unbranched cylindrical hallow tube. It is covered in tiny hairs making it appear almost translucent. It's fun to plait or on the beach, a long length can be used as skipping rope. It may look a little like spaghetti (sea spaghetti has forked fronds) but in my opinion it doesn't taste as nice. Some eat *C. filum* which can be cooked in noodle fashion, the younger the better.

Sea Rocket
Cakile maritima

This perennial, low growing herb looks pretty in sand dunes and on the splash zone of the beach, where its thick, fleshy leaves have adapted to tolerate both sea spray and blown sand. In the Hebrides the taproot plants are often covered by windswept sand, but it seems to have no adverse effect. Historically, in times of famine, the roots of sea rocket were ground and the powder used to make bread. It is reputed to be rich in Vitamin C and when it is young, you might grab your vitamin burst by eating its succulent upper stems. The overpowering taste is of horseradish or mustard,

Sea rocket *(Cakile maritima)*

although blanching or steaming removes some of the pungency. As with many steamed sea vegetables it reaches another level when liberally smeared with butter. Young sea rocket leaves taste peppery and may be added to salads, but I finely shred larger leaves or smear the juice around the salad bowl. A little sea rocket goes a long way. I was keen to create a recipe where sea rocket adds to a dish, and was delighted to discover that the mauve flowers turn rice vinegar pink. As with all flowers in the *brassicaceae* (mustard) family, they are cross-shaped with four petals in opposite pairs. The sea rocket flower adds colour and interest, rather than an overpowering bitter twist to herb vinegar. Sea rocket is in flower from June to August, although some stragglers may bloom on into autumn. If you forget to take the pepper pot to the beach, a well-wiped sea rocket leaf will come to your aid. In late summer the seeds will add a mustardy kick to your cooking. Less is definitely more.

Green Seaweeds
Ulva spp

Green seaweeds are found on both sandy and rocky beaches. Many can tolerate low salinity and will colonise areas where rivers meet the sea. The green colour of the seaweed is due to the green pigment chlorophyll, required for the photosynthesis of light.

Using only chlorophyll means that green seaweeds require decent levels of light. They will not thrive in shadowed areas or water that is too deep. It gives them the ability to thrive higher up the shore without competition from the red or brown seaweeds. These are flat or tubular green seaweeds and look very similar. To date, there are around thirteen listed species of *ulva* for Britain, five are blade forming (as sea lettuce) and the rest are tubular. Because of the variable shape they are difficult to identify without the help of a microscope. Professor Mike Guiry suggests that molecular work is the only reliable way of identifying leafy *Ulvas*, and notes it a ridiculous situation. I refer to them as *ulva*. Often species can only be identified under a microscope, but all are edible. Sea lettuce (*Ulva lactuca*) is emerald green and two cells thick. At times it can be almost translucent and tear easily. It looks like a damp, version of the common or garden round lettuce. Sea lettuce favours fresh water seepage, so if harvesting for culinary use avoid sea lettuce loitering near outflows on the upper shore. Sea lettuce is also fond of mud flats and, as a lightweight, is easily pulled from its holdfast by wave force. Don't pick floating lettuce because it may have floated through polluted waters or have 'sailed' for days. It grows rapidly and in the summer months may form a green tide. My favourite place to pick sea lettuce is in rock pools on the lower shore, where it mixes with other red and brown seaweeds, but is easily distinguishable by its bright colour. As it floats underwater it is easy to cut and will be sand free, when popped in a bag.

GUTWEED
Ulva intestinalis

Ulva intestinalis is known as maiden's hair, gutweed (which doesn't sound very appetizing), green mermaid's hair or sea grass, which certainly sounds more appetising. It is found in high shore pools, where it rapidly carpets large areas of rock or sand. Where it is very abundant, it can, like sea lettuce, cause pollution problems. In 2009

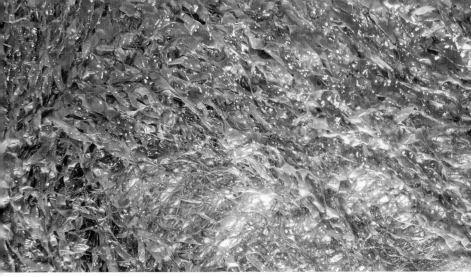

Gutweed or green maiden's hair and knotted wrack. Tubular Ulva, **formerly called** *Enteromorpha*

over a hundred beaches in Brittany were closed due to sea lettuce carpets or green tides. As the seaweed decomposes hydrogen sulphide is given off. Holidaymakers do not appreciate the stench.

DOUBLE RIBBON WEED
Ulva linza

Another very similar species, which is common on rocks in the middle to sub-tidal zone is doubled ribbon weed (*Ulva linza*). Its base is tubular, but it is flattened at the top. In many ways it is a good cross between sea lettuce and gutweed.

ULVA KNOW HOW

The emerald green body has a crumple frond, which looks like a lettuce leaf but can be up to 20 cm in length and more in width. It is best to pick small fronds of sea lettuce from the intertidal zone, in clean rock pools far away from fear of any fresh water seepage.

Gutweed, in common with sea lettuce, enjoys freshwater drainage, so a word of caution before picking. Picked from a clean habitat, however, it is a nutritious food which can be eaten raw or cooked. It is emerald green and its long and tubular frond can grow up to 30 cm in length. After washing to remove sand, shredded *Ulva spp* are delicious in a stir-fry. For

Green Sponge Fingers, *Codium fragile* **in sandy rock pools**

my recipes, I'm happy to mix and match *Ulva spp* depending on the pickings of the day. There is usually such an abundance of these seaweeds that careful picking isn't an issue. However, the holdfast is tiny. It may be less than a strand of hair in thickness, so use scissors to cut it.

GREEN SPONGE FINGERS
Codium fragile & Codium tomentosum

Green Sponge Fingers *Codium fragile* and *Codium tomentosum* are very tricky to distinguish between. Twenty species of *Codium* are currently recorded in the marine algal flora of Korea (Kim et al. 2013), and some of these species are considered invasive i.e. introduced. Seaweed cooks will be happy to leave classification to the academics. In 1930, William Setchell, Professor of Botany at the University of California, wrote of this species in a letter to Arthur Cotton, the keeper of the herbarium at Kew Gardens: 'In all probability this species is simply a depauperate form of your variety.' The acronym *ssp* in contemporary seaweed guides denotes a subspecies, suggesting that there is still much difficulty in identification. Green Sponge Fingers may also be called velvet horn, dead man's fingers, seastag horn or Atlantic green sponge fingers. Its spongy texture is reminiscent of the felt covering on a billiard table. Interestingly, *Codium fragile spp fragile* has been used by the pharmaceutical industry as an anticoagulant, which is noteworthy because most of the seaweeds used within industry are brown or red. In Korea *codium* is harvested from the wild and sold in local markets. It is also used as insect repellant. Atlantic green sponge fingers (*C. fragile spp atlanticum*) is considered to be native to Britain and fragile green sponge fingers (*C. fragile ssp fragile*) non-native. The latter, i.e. the non-native species, is more common.

GREEN SPONGE FINGERS / VELVET HORN KNOW HOW
The *Codium spp* provide sea vegetable bulk and dry well. This seaweed doesn't freeze. The author V.J. Chapman suggests that it should be collected in April and May, and then dried and preserved in ash or salt. In Japan seaweed is often salted, but I have not tested this idea. If this seaweed is said to resemble a dead man's fingers, it also looks like a deer's antler. It is found in rock pools, and on open rock on the lower shore and sub-tidal. The spongy fronds are long and its large holdfast is easy for a harvester to avoid. It's the largest of the green seaweeds. This species could not be described as 'slimy' seaweed; its texture is captured in the word 'velvet' of its name. Where velvet horn grows prolifically it has a substantial feel to it, and is a useful sea vegetable when you are feeding large numbers. One of my favourite ways to cook velvet horn is in a tempura batter or with potatoes in a *Dauphinoise*.

WILD SALAD LEAVES

From spring to early autumn, armed with a pocket guide to help with identification, the coastal cook may gather salad leaves as he or she wanders along the shoreline. Here are some of the delicious leaves that you may, if you don't pay attention, tread upon:

SCURVY GRASS
Cochlearia officinalis

Long before the word vitamin was associated with nutrients and health, this coastal plant was given to sailors to help fight the disease scurvy. A member of the *brassicaceae* family, it is not unlike watercress in taste and appearance. The first white flowers show in spring and its succulent leaves add a mustard piquancy to a salad, and they work as a garnish too. Sea purslane (*Atriplex portulacoides*) is a pleasant, cloudy green summer plant found on salt marshes. The leaves may be used in a salad and are also delicious in pesto. It may be confused with sea sandwort (*Honckenya peploides*), the tender leaves of which can be picked in early spring. The young edible asparagus style shoots of sea mayweed (*Tripleurospermum maritimum ssp*) also work well in salads. Its daisy-like flower makes it an easily recognisable plant. Scotch lovage (*Ligusticum scoticum*) is a stocky coastal version of the garden variety with a strong aromatic taste of celery. It should be used sparingly. If you can safely identify umbellifers (some are toxic) the leaves of seashore wild angelica (*Angelica sylvestris*) make a wonderful addition to a seaside salad. Pretty angelica blushes pink and decks coastal cliffs; both its leaves and stems are delicious. The stalks may be steamed or candied. My mother used angelica in floral designs on trifles in the 1970s. Candied, the stalk will add a retro twist to a dull cupcake.

From spring to early summer the inconspicuous wild sorrel (*Rumex acetosa*) is at its best. The Latin for the family name *Rumex* translates as 'I suck', and this is exactly what generations of children have done to sorrel, to quench their thirst. Sorrel is a member of the dock family. Its smaller, lemon/sour apple tasting leaves are not dissimilar to the astringent, stocky docken used to soothe nettle stings. Docks are harmless if eaten but lack the Haribo sour buzz of sorrel. Sorrel is found on damp pathways and sneaks into crevices on coastal cliffs. The herbalists and early physicians are full of praise for sorrel. Sorrel predates lemons and does much the same job. Sorrel leaves soaked in boiling water produce pink liquid – add sugar to make delicious sorrel syrup, which when caramelised can be used in crème caramel. Sorrel is very acidic and is used as a rennet substitute to sour milk in cheese making. It is a useful cook's herb.

Collect some seaside leaves; add chopped sea lettuce instead of salt, sea rocket in place of pepper and sorrel to replace vinegar. Drizzle with oil, and you have a seasoned beach salad.

Wireweed
Sargassum muticum

Wireweed also known as japweed, is a fast growing species. It was first noted in Britain in 1971 on the Isle of Wight. Wireweed grows in the shallow sub-tidal and rock pools, where it competes with native species for light. It wins. In summer wireweed can grow up to 10 cm a day and has a relatively long life of three to four years. This encourages dense matting, which may impact on oyster beds and other aquaculture. Marine scientists note increasing boundaries of wireweed populations, and are watchful of its competition with native species such as sea oak and oarweed. Professor Mike Guiry says that 'the loss of a frond is not fatal to the weed because it can grow from the remaining primary axis, often buried in sand or debris'. Wireweed is highly fecund and a floating frond can survive for up to three months. It has yet to invade the isle of South Uist. I purchased dried wireweed for recipe testing because it is seasonal and dies back in the autumn, so can't be harvested over winter months. Chinese Traditional Medicine uses seaweed as a principle ingredient, to which herbalists add compatible herbs tailored to a patient's needs. *Hai zao* (*Sargassum spp*) is commonly used in prescriptions. In 2004, the Food Standards Agency advised consumers not to eat a related species, *Hijiki*

Sargassum fusiforme because of accumulated levels of inorganic arsenic. This was refuted in *The Japan Times*. To my knowledge there is no health worry about the consumption of wireweed.

Wireweed, as is the case with many invasive types of seaweed, isn't particularly fussy where it grows, and it adapts to a lack of sunlight, desiccation and water salinity. It is light brown with small, yellow-brown, iridescent cylindrical air bladders. The bladders resemble small grapes and sit on short stalks. The fronds can grow up to 2 m in length. Floating manes of wireweed will carpet large areas. If you cut wireweed, harvest it with care to ensure that you don't leave floating fronds, which may move on and reproduce.

Hawaiians have five species of *Sargassum spp* to cook with and many traditional recipes to choose from. A quick perusal of a Hawaiian website or cookery book will be valuable for wireweed cooks. Some recipes include raw seaweed and octopus, which may not be to everyone's taste, but others are exciting. I connected the delicious pairing of coconut milk with seaweed after looking at Hawaiian recipes online – the resulting panna cotta was delicious.

WRACKS

The distribution of the fucoids is affected by substratum (for anchorage), exposure to wave action, the angle of the slope of the shore, salinity and tidal range. However, as you go down to the sea, there is an order in which you will slip over the wracks. They are tricky to identify, but the beach zones are helpful.

CHANNEL WRACK
Pelvetia canaliculata

The first that you will tread upon is channel wrack, or cow tang, so named because it is found where cattle feed. Some authors may refer to this as channelled wrack. Channel wrack has its own distinctive zone. High shore species are black and brittle and look unappetising, lower down the shore the wrack becomes olive in colour and these fronds are worth picking. Channel wrack has curved fronds (the channel), which help to retain moisture by trapping water. Swollen lumps at the tip of the fronds contain its reproductive structures. It doesn't have bladders. Channel wrack lives for about four years and can survive lower nutrient levels than other seaweeds because it recovers from water loss rapidly (desiccation). It may lose 90 % of its water and yet rehydrate within twenty minutes when covered with seawater. Channel wrack is a good indicator of the high water mark. It is one of the seaweeds reported to produce chloroform naturally. I wonder if the Victorian phychologist Margaret Gatty, who was one of the first Sheffield ladies to be given chloroform during childbirth, was aware of this.

SPIRALLED WRACK
Fucus spiralis

Spiralled wrack is an upper shore weed which has a mid-rib, but no bladders, and covers rocks high up on sheltered shores. It can survive for long periods of time out of the water and marks the high water mark of neap tides. It grows in a band below channel wrack.

ASCO
Ascophyllum nodosum

Asco may also be referred to as egg wrack, rock weed, sea whistle, yellow tang or Norwegian kelp. It's useful because it can be harvested all year around. Growth is at its slowest in winter and fastest in April and May, but decreases during long periods of sunshine. Most research suggests that the species has a long life span of twenty years, but other papers suggest upwards of fifty years.

Bladder wracks

The wracks provide an important winter fodder for livestock, and in parts of Scotland sheep continue to graze on seaweed. In 1745, Linnaeus reported on the mixing of boiled bladder wrack with bran to produce pig food on North Ronaldsay (Orkney). In 2005 a cluster of orthostatic stones was exposed by coastal erosion at Meur on the Orcadian Isle of Sanday. The subsequent excavation revealed a burnt mound which was occupied between the late second millennium and mid-first millennium. It was used for cooking. Although it was primarily fuelled by peat, charred seaweed was found by the archaeology team. There is no evidence that seaweed was used as an ingredient, but of course it is eaten by North Ronaldsay sheep. These sheep are still fed exclusively on seaweed for ten months of the year, only being put onto pasture during the lambing season. The sheep are predominately fed on the storm cast kelps, and have been the subject of studies researching inorganic arsenic. The question asked is whether the North Ronaldsay sheep have developed a new way to detoxify arsenic; to date it has not been answered. The lamb is much sought after by butchers.

The fronds of asco are long, slender and branched with interspersed ovoid air bladders, which vary in size. Given some regularity of bladder size it is not unlike a necklace. Its age can be estimated by counting the number of bladders on a frond: an air bladder is produced at the tip of a frond annually. Age may, however, be underestimated because there is no guarantee that it will produce a bladder in the early years. Asco is the largest of the wracks and grows abundantly on sheltered shores to the exclusion of other species. It will densely carpet large areas of the middle shore and also grow in sea lochs. Asco is the dominant species of the sheltered and semi exposed intertidal zone.

BLADDER WRACK
Fucus vesiculosus

Bladder wrack may also be known as lady wrack, button seaweed, kelpware or pigweed. This is found in the intertidal zone on rocky shores, often near knotted wrack. It has a mid-rib and round blister air bladders, which are often paired. Some argue that the bladders lift the seaweed towards the light. Older, larger fronds have more bladders, but heavy wave battering may thwart bladder growth.

SERRATED WRACK
Fucus serratus

Serrated wrack is sometimes referred to as toothed wrack, saw wrack or notched wrack. This seaweed has flat fronds with a mid-rib and the edges of the fronds are serrated or jagged. It is often found in a distinct shore zone below knotted wrack and bladder wrack. It does not have air bladders and is found on sheltered coasts in the intertidal zone. It is the preferred seaweed of those involved in thalassotherapy and the cosmetic industry.

Serrated wrack (Fucus serratus)

In autumn serrated wrack produces small nodules at the tips of the blades, these are reproductive vessels which are then shed. At this point foliage is lost and the wrack reduces in size considerably.

COOKING THE WRACKS

I tend to interchange the wracks in recipes as I have them to hand. Fresh fronds respond to slow cooking. Once dried, the wracks can be used for seasoning and make very good stock. Traditionally serrated wrack has been used as a tea, but if I had to name my favourite tea, it is made with dried velvet horn.

'Common Objects at the Seaside' by John Leech, Punch, 1857

CHAPTER FOUR

HISTORY

Seaweeds have long been used in food diets as well as traditional remedies in East Asia. Today, in the Western Hemisphere, seaweeds are essentially valued for their phycocolloid contents. Phycocolloid is a generic name used to identify the water-soluble polysaccharides produced by seaweeds. These macromolecules are widely used in food, cosmetic and biotechnology industries for their gelling, stabilizing and thickening properties. Agar, carrageenan, and alginates that are extracted from red and brown seaweeds, are the three main principals of phycocolloids.

The oldest documented use of seaweed for human consumption dates back to Monte Verde, from an archeological site in southern Chile. The uncovering of remnants of nine species of algae, including partially burned or squashed fragments on stone tools, in the Monte Verde site in the late 1970s, attests to the early settlement of South America along the Pacific coast. It also suggests that seaweeds were important to the diet and health of early humans in the Americas at least 14,600 years ago. In addition, academics now propose that inland Native American populations might have used some of these coastal species as goods for trading, leading to a theory that kelp forest ecosystems may have provided a kind of 'kelp highway' for early maritime peoples colonizing the New World.

In the *Shijing,* the earliest collection of Chinese poetry compiled during the time of Confucius, there is a poem that describes a housewife cooking seaweed, which suggests that seaweed was eaten at this period. Representations of seaweed were put on roof beams in Chinese houses, because it was believed that seaweed, as a water plant, could repel the fire spirit. Indeed, seaweed bungalows are still part of the architecture in Rongcheng, Shandong province. During the Song Dynasty (960-1279) laver or nori (*Porphyra spp*), from the Haitan Island in Fujian province, was presented annually to the Emperor. Seaweed gains yet more kudos by its inclusion on the 'five-clawed dragon robes' worn by the Emperor. It was one of the Twelve Symbols of Sovereignty, and represented purity.

Seaweed had of course long been a revered food item: in 600 BCE, the Chinese philosopher Sze Teu wrote, 'Some algae are a delicacy fit for the most honoured guests, even for the King himself.' In Tonga, people are reputed to have eaten a brown seaweed, 'Limu moui', for at least 3000 years, and some believe it is responsible for their remarkable longevity and good health. When Captain Cook visited Tonga in 1777 he was said to have been given Limu moui to restore his strength and energy.

The Japanese love affair with nori is well known, if only through sushi, but the Japanese affection for the British phycologist, Dr Kathleen Mary Drew (1901-57) is less widely recognised. In Japan Drew is known as 'Mother of the Sea'. In 1949, she published a very brief note in the scientific journal, *Nature,* entitled 'Conchocelis-Phase in the Life History of *Porphyra umbilicalis*', which Goran Michanek, in his biographical study of Drew, described as '100 lines that should change the world'. Kathleen Drew identified the missing link in the life cycle of *porphyra.* Heteromorphy is the alteration of generations, which means that in the case of *porphyra* it takes on different appearances during its life cycle. Prior to her discovery, *porphyra* life stages were thought to be two different species. Drew's research (and subsequent work by Japanese academics and seaweed farmers) changed the way that laver or nori was cultivated, and resulted in a guaranteed harvest. Previously, harvests were unpredicatable, and as a consequence nori was known as 'gamblers' grass'. Grateful nori farmers contributed posthumously to a statue in Drew's honour, and each year on 14 April (her birthday) a festival is celebrated in her memory in Sumiyoshi Shrine Park. Kathleen Drew was also the first president of the British Phycological Society.

Dr Kathleen Mary Drew (1901-57)

The earliest recorded use of seaweed in Britain can be found in a poem in *A Celtic Psaltery.* It is attributed to St Columba (521-597), and references the monks of Iona collecting dulse from the rocks:

What greater joy could be?
Now plucking dulse upon the rocky shore,
Now fishing eager on,
Now furnishing food unto the famished poor

Writing in 1703, the teacher and author Martin Martin, a Gael, noted that in the Outer Hebrides an offering of the fruits of the land (porridge, mead or ale) was poured into the sea as a sacrifice to the sea god Shony, in the hope that seaweed (manure) would be plentiful. The ceremony was reputed to have begun in St Mulvay (*St Moluag*) Church in Port of Ness on the Isle of Lewis, and the sea deity was toasted thus: 'Shony I give you this cup of ale, hoping that you'll be so kind as to send us plenty of sea ware (seaweed), for enriching the ground the ensuing year.' Although Martin Martin described the ceremony as 'a ridiculous piece of superstition' that had been 'quite abolished for these 32 years past', the rite later resurfaced as part of Maundy Thursday customs on the Isle of Lewis and took the form of the following prayer:

Oh God of the sea,
Put weed in the drawing wave
To enrich the ground
To shower us with food.

There are many Hogmanay rites and superstitions and some include the 'Flo'er of the Shore'. In the north east of Scotland farmers compete for the first load of 'sea ware' from the shore on New Year's morning. The lucky one placed a little seaweed at each door in the farm steading, and put a portion in each field to ensure a prosperous year. Sea ware is still used as manure. On New Year's walks on the Isle of South Uist, I often see crofters in tractors on the beach, filling their trailers with seaweed. Alexander Carmichael, in his *Carmina Gadelica: Hymns and Incantations* (1928), records a Gaelic prayer giving thanks for an abundance of seaweed:

Come and come is seaweed,
Come and come is red sea-ware
Come is yellow weed, come is tangle,
Come is food, which the wave enwraps

In *A Description of the Western Isles of Scotland* (1703), Martin Martin writes of 'the remarkable Cures perform'd by the Natives merely by the Ufe of simples...*Linarich* [which I think is the Ulva species], a very thin fmall green Plant...is apply'd Plaifter-wife to the Forehead and Temples, to produce Sleep for fuch as have a Fever, and they fay it is effectual for this purpofe'. He continues: '*Dulse*...is very good for the sight; but if boil'd, it proves more loofening, if the juice be drank with it.' He also notes that 'it kills Worms' and that 'the Natives eat it boil'd with Butter, and reckon it very wholefom. The *Dulfe* recommended here, is that which grows on Stone, and not that which grows on the *Alga Marina*, or *Sea-Tangle*; for tho that be likewife eaten, it will not ferve in any of the Cafes above mention'd'. Of sea tangle (*Laminaria spp*) Martin writes, 'the Blade is eat by the vulgar Natives. I had an account of a young Man who had loft his Appetite, and taken Pills to no purpofe; and being advis'd to boil the Blade of the *Alga* and drink the Infufion boil'd with a little Butter, was reftor'd to his former State of Health'.

As with many traditional practices, modern science is working to explain, post facto, why the ancients may have been right in associating seaweed with medicinal and health benefits. Hebrideans cooked seaweed, but also used leftover ashes from burning kelp to flavour cheese if salt was in short supply. The filamentous seaweeds were used in ropes, fishing lines and nets, and kelp stipes provided natural lye for artisan soap makers.

The east coast of Scotland is steeped in dulse history. In 1651, after the execution of Charles I, the Scottish regalia (crown, sceptre and sword) were removed to Dunnotar Castle, a clifftop fortress in Kincardineshire, to avoid the marauding Cromwell and his troops. When the location was discovered, legend says that the crown jewels were lowered down the castle rock to a fishwife or servant girl who, on pretence of gathering 'tangles' on the seashore, carried them off, hidden under the dulse in her creel. The Revd Grainger then buried the regalia under the floor of his kirk, where it remained hidden until the restoration of King Charles II in 1660. The jewels were then returned to Edinburgh.

Seaweeds are also mentioned in the nineteenth century weekly magazine, *Household Words,* which was edited by Charles Dickens. In 1856, John Robertson, an Aberdonian contributor to the magazine, wrote warmly of dulse being 'a regular relish on the tables of all ranks in Aberdeen, my native town'. By contrast, it is interesting to note that the eighteenth-century Cornish marine algae expert, John Stackhouse, deemed dulse only fit to be eaten by the less affluent. In his *Household Words* article, entitled 'The Purple Shore', Robertson splendidly described the Aberdeen 'dulse-wives' and noted their persuasive bids to encourage a small boy to part with his *bawbee* (Scottish halfpenny):

When I was a boy, from half-a-dozen to a dozen dulse-wives, according to the season, used to sit every morning on the paving stones of the Castlegate selling dulse…Dressed in clean white mutches, or caps, with silk-handkerchiefs spread over their breasts, and blue stuff wrappers and petticoats, the ruddy and sonsie dulse-women looked the types of health and strength. Every dulse-wife had a clean white cloth spread half over the mouth of her creel at the side furthest from her, and nearest her customers. The cloth served as a counter on which the dulse was heaped into the handkerchiefs of the purchasers. Many a time, when my whole weekly income was a halfpenny, a Friday's bawbee, I have expended it on dulse, in preference to apples, pears, blackberries, cranberries, strawberries, wild peas and sugar-sticks. When I approached, there used to be quite a competition among the dulse-wives for my bawbee. The young ones looked most winning, and the old ones cracked the best jokes. A young one would say: 'Come to me, bonnie laddie, and I'll gie ye mair for yer bawbee than any o' them.' An old one would say: 'Come to me, laddie, an I'll tell what like yer wife will be.'

Further down the east coast in Auchmithie, Margaret Horn regularly offered carrageen pudding and dulse on the menu of her acclaimed seafood restaurant, The But'n'Ben. It was, however, her dulse tale that made me smile. As a child, she remembered the landlords of Dundee public houses piling dulse high on the bar for customers to toast and nibble upon. Her eyes twinkled as she told me the publican's reasoning – dulse made the customers thirsty and encouraged replenishment of glasses. Bartenders in Ireland were wise to this idea too. The 'tang' in the Edinburgh street sellers' cry, 'Who'll buy my dulse and tang?', refers to sugar kelp which, like dulse, was eaten as a snack. As late as 1950, tiny restaurants in the Hilltown area of Dundee called *caookies*, served a popular delicacy of tripe and tatties with dulse.

There has been a recent discovery of nineteenth-century nautical charts depicting hand drawn illustrations of kelp beds in British Columbia. Kelp was considered a navigational hazard, and as a consequence carefully highlighted in nautical maps by the British Navy. These charts will be helpful to contemporary scientists who are concerned about kelp growth as sea water temperatures rise. The historic nautical maps can be compared with satellite images in order to monitor kelp bed growth.

Belief and Natural History

The earliest attempt to divide algae into a greater number of genera was by a Scot, the Revd Dr John Walker. Walker was holder of the Regius Chair of Natural History and Keeper of the Museum of Natural History in the University of Edinburgh, from 1779 until his death in 1803. Interestingly, he also found time to be Moderator of the General Assembly of the Church of Scotland. Perhaps this is a digression, but one which is fascinating because many seaweed enthusiasts were clerics or the wives of clergy. This is not surprising perhaps because the aim underlying early Victorian natural history books (of which there were many) was the desire to show evidence of God's existence via natural theology. Although a fundamental belief was that everything God had created was for man's convenience and that there was no need to prove it, there was a need to 'prove' that a species was good or useful to man. In his book *Glaucus, or The Wonders of the Shore* (1855), Charles Kingsley's pays homage to the burgeoning interest in marine natural history. (It was Kingsley who coined the word 'pteridomania', a combination of *pterido* – Latin for fern – and mania, to refer to the contemporary craze for collecting ferns). In the book, Kingsley describes seaweeds and molluscs that can be seen around the south coast of England. He found inspiration in Philip Henry Gosse's books *A Naturalist's Rambles on the Devonshire Coast* (1853) and *The Aquarium* (1854). However, the two men would later differ in options on geological timescales and evolution. During the 1830s to 1850s Charles Lyell's geological theory that the fossil records revealed a continual birth and extinction of species caused controversy. Gosse, a literalist who believed in the Biblical creation story, produced a theory that fossils and strata preexisted i.e. that they had been put on earth by the creator in order to suggest that the earth had a prior history. This debate, stimulated by Lyell's new theory, prepared the way for Darwinism. Kingsley remained a creationist, but suggested that organisms could change under the control of their creator. However, he accepted the possibility of evolution and was sympathetic to the ideas set out by Charles Darwin in *On the Origin of Species* (1859). Unlike Gosse, Kingsley appears to have been flexible and felt no need to prove that everything in nature was created for the benefit of man. He cited a lack of biblical reference to support his view, and saw little in Darwinism that he could not be reconciled with his own beliefs. The creation debate must have confused the Victorian layman who collected fossils on a Saturday and read Genesis in church the following day. Creationism continues to cause conflict.

Cornwall also claims a marine algae expert by the name of John Stackhouse, a classicist who was interested in botany. Stackhouse built Acton Castle so that he could have easy access to study seaweed in what has become known as Stackhouse Cove. He saw seaweed as a beautiful but neglected flora. Special baths were let into the floor of the castle, so that he could keep specimens fresh as he drew and studied them. These drawings were published in his book *Nereis Britannica, or a Botanical Description of British Marine Plants* (1797), and in the preface Stackhouse described the method he used for preparing and preserving specimens of seaweed. Cornwall continued to attract sea floral specialists during the Victorian era. There is mention of a Cornish black butter, not of the kind referred to by Mrs Beeton or Jane Austen, but made from the seaweed, laver. Stackhouse noted that only the poor ate it. Many country lanes in the West of England are called 'Donkey Lane' and this dates back to the days when donkeys hauled seaweed from the coast to agricultural land. Seaweed is still used on the land in Cornwall, and many follow the old practice in which seaweed is mixed with sand, left to rot and then dug into the soil. Seaweed protects thin sandy soil and minimises wind erosion. The alginate in seaweed binds the soil together, moistens it and also adds valuable nutrients.

Laver is one of Britain's better-known seaweeds. Martin Martin said that it was the only food that a human needed to survive, while Dorothy Hartley wrote that it was a fashionable delicacy sold by 'laver women' in the streets of Bath, where 'fine potted laver', was a common street cry. This points to geographical markets beyond Wales, where laver is renowned. In spa towns it was sold as a restorative for ailing bodies, as well as a victual. Hartley also writes that 'our Anglo Saxon forefathers used it as a cure for the stone in the bladder'. Laver, although traditionally associated with the Gower coastline in Wales, has been hawked in streets and eaten in Britain for hundreds of years. The Revd Nicholas Roberts, rector of Lhan Dhewi Velfrey in Pembrokeshire, described the process of turning laver into laverbread in a letter quoted in Edmund Gibson's edition of *Camden's Britannia* (1772):

Having gathered the weed, they wash it clean from sand an slime and sweat it between two tile-stones, then they shred it small and knead it well, as they do dough for bread, and make it up into great balls or rolls, which some eat raw others fry'd with oatmeal and butter. It is accounted sovereign against all distempers of the liver and spleen...

It is therefore only to be expected that laverbread (*bara lawr*) is a strong survivor of traditional regional cooking. The Welsh breakfast dish is made by simmering well-washed laver for hours until it is tender and resembles a thick, gelatinous olive green paste. This is mixed with oatmeal, rolled into flat cakes and lightly fried. Miners are reported to have eaten *bara lawr* with cockles, but this must have been dependent on the geographical location of the coal pit. Laver is also known as *black caviar*, a name which perhaps has its origin in coalmining, though laver enthusiasts of today may dispute this. The nineteenth-century wandering author George Borrow mentions a piping hot laver sauce, served with moor mutton in his book *Wild Wales: Its People, Language and Scenery* (1862). Further afield, the renowned chef of that era, Alexis Soyer, served laver as a delicacy in the London Reform Club where it was presented in a silver saucepan, garnished with lemons to flank a roast leg of mutton. More recently, on the Pembrokeshire coast, a small thatched seaweed hut has been restored as an example of a seaweed-drying hut. At the height of the laverbread industry there were huts the length of the Pembrokeshire coast, each one maintained by a family in cottage industry style. In common with many coastal communities, the men went deep-sea fishing leaving the women to gather cockles, mussels and seaweed. Dylan Thomas writes of 'web-footed cockle women'. The womenfolk were tough. The laver was dried in the huts before being sent to market, or to Swansea for processing. Laver was also sold to Derbyshire coalfield areas, where it was thought to benefit goitre. Welsh mothers admonished their children with the words 'eat your laverbread or you'll get Derbyshire neck'. Laver is sometimes referred to as the 'Weed of Hiraeth', *hiraeth* being the Welsh concept of nostalgia or longing for home.

Laver also had a West Country commercial heritage, where fine potted laver was hawked through the streets of Jane Austen's eighteenth-century Bath. Further west in Devon, it was prepared by the wives of fishermen and sold as a prepared ingredient in fish or butchers' shops. In Devon and Cornwall laver is still eaten at breakfast with the traditional white spicy sausage, called Hog's pudding. In Scotland sailors would make a sloke jelly, which they took to sea and ate with oatcakes. The value of laver in helping to prevent sailors from contracting scurvy on long sea voyages is well documented.

Scottish and Irish recipes often use carrageen in a blancmange-like pudding, but historically it was given as a tonic to consumptives. Soaked in honey and warm milk, it was offered to children as a cough remedy. Medical herbalists continue to prescribe carrageen for bronchial conditions and peptic ulcers. Dorothy Hartley refers to it as 'Dorset weed' and recalls it being hung to dry in bags in Cerne Abbas. After noting that, as with terrestrial plants, there is a season for gathering seaweed, Hartley describes washing the collected carrageen in running brook water and leaving it to dry on the grass. The chemist, she states, knew it as 'Iberian moss' and used it in emulsions. Among her list of its uses Hartley notes that it 'fixes false teeth'. Writing in an era when many would have had teeth removed as a twenty-first-birthday gift, I suspect that this was as relevant as its use today in toothpaste. Continuing the over-21 theme, one of Jamaica's notorious aphrodisiac drinks, which is deemed to put 'lead in your pencil', includes carrageen. Jamaican Irish Moss drink recipes vary, but each contains carrageen, most include condensed milk, and some will add rum. The added spice extras are down to personal taste. Irish migrants are held responsible for the introduction of carrageen to Jamaica and therein the development of the drink. My favourite use of carrageen is in a large Vermont house, where a thick layer of dried *Chondrus crispus* was put underneath a dance floor to reduce impact trauma to dancing couples' feet.

Amateurs may muddle between carrageen species, but for the cook it is about gelling properties. I find that grape pip weed produces the firmest set. Carrageen differences are contrasted in John Robertson's article 'The Purple Shore', which appeared in *Household Words*:

> *The common plants which appear best to identify the purple zone are the two well-known gristly weeds sold as Irish moss, which are eaten by the wise in the shape of jellies and blancmanges. The colour of both is purple. The Irish moss of the shops, or carrageen of the Irish, is called by the savans* Chondrus crispus *or the curly gristle. The blade is variable in breadth – gristly, branching doubly, flat or curly, with wedgelike segments, and tops that seem to be broken off. A gristly plant popularly confounded with the curly gristle, is called, by the learned,* Gigartina mamillosa. *Ladies who have studied these plants with culinary views, prefer the* Gigartina mamillosa *to the* Chondrus crispus.

This confirms my belief that I obtain a better set when cooking with *Gigartina mamillosa*. As with many other revisions in the world of seaweed, this is now known by the Latin name *Mastocarpus stellatus* and by the common name grape pip weed. Robertson refers to ladies with culinary views, but many Victorian authors of general books about seaweed were also female. Louisa Lane Clarke's *Common Seaweeds of the British Coast and Channel Islands* (1865) includes a study of the Channel Islands, where there is a long history of harvesting seaweed.

Early records dated 1299 note that in the Channel Islands,

'vraic' (the Jersey dialect word for seaweed) was a frequent cause of quarrels and criminal charges in the Royal Court. In the late sixteenth century, when ecclesiastical law was as important as secular, parish farmers were given exact dates on which vraic might be cut in allocated zones of the shoreline. A hundred years later restrictions were placed on knitting, an activity that occupied a great many Channel Island households, to ensure that vraicing was not interrupted. For centuries 'vraitcheurs' relied on horses and carts, in particularly the 'hernais', a two-wheeled conveyance with no springs, which is often portrayed in paintings by the Jersey artist, Edmund Blampied. Harvesting vraic was dangerous work, and early Jersey death registers refer to drowning while harvesting seaweed. In *An Account of the Island of Jersey* (1813), under a heading entitled 'Manure, wrack, called vraic, and vraicing', William Pleece writes that seaweed was important not only as a fertiliser, but for heating fuel too. Henry Inglis, writing in 1834, notes a communal and commendable attitude to harvesting: 'The evening before that appointed for the vraic gathering, the church bell rings at six o'clock; which is the signal for all who are interested in vraic gathering – all the inhabitants of the island who are owners of land – to assemble in the church-yard; and there, the important point is discussed, whether all are ready to commence the next morning. Any sufficient cause that might prevent any one individual from joining in the vraic-gathering would be held a sufficient reason for postponing the day; because the liberty of gathering vraic is too valuable a privilege, to be unequally enjoyed.'

A Jersey cake, called *galettes à vrai* or vraic bun, was specially baked for the 'vraiccers', but alas, the buns contained raisins not seaweed. In 'Jersey Jottings', published in a Jersey newspaper in 1862, the vraic bun was described as : 'Not at all a rich morsel, the "Vraicking biscuit" is anything but a depisable [*sic*] one, and being at once sweet and wholesome, is famous "plenishing" for a hungry man's stomach'. A bun providing energy for vraicing was probably more relevant than whether it contained seaweed, but I confess to feeling disappointment. Vehicles are now involved in vraicing, but vraic is still spread on potatoes and is interwoven with the early history of the Jersey potato. Seaweed could only be collected from Jersey's beaches at certain times of the year and never on a Sunday due to the law. This posed a problem for those who harvested seaweed commercially. A new law called the 'Aquatic Resources (Jersey) Law' was sanctioned on 20 June 2014. This means that vraic may now be harvested with business acumen.

The Channel Island seaweed author Louise Lane Clarke, who was the granddaughter of a governor of Alderney, also published *Folk-lore of Guernsey and Sark* (1880). Clarke, the wife of an English vicar and an expert botanist, was a part of a Victorian literary world which sought health and well-being through their love of nature. Focusing on objects of God's natural beauty such as seaweed served as a displacement activity for life's pressures and difficulties.

In *A Popular History of British Sea-Weeds* (1857), the first of many Victorian seaweed books, the Revd David Landsborough suggested that fifty years prior to the publication of his book seaweed was treated with disdain. These books were not for specialists but for lovers of the richness of natural history. Landsborough was both academic and enterprising in his appreciation of seaweed, but ladies are central to any Victorian study of seaweed. I shall concentrate on Great Britain but seaweed had a similar female cult following in America.

Codium fragile (Green Sponge fingers)

CHAPTER FIVE

THE SEAWEED SISTERHOOD

Until the mid-nineteenth century, female interest in natural history had been mainly confined to botany, but about this time an enthusiasm for shells, seaweeds, ferns, fossils, animals and plants entered the parlour cabinets of curiosity. Ladies collected and pressed specimens, and enjoyed the natural world as much as their male counterparts. Many middle-class Victorian women were trained to draw with precision, and their drawings would be used to illustrate the texts written by their male partners, though the fact was not always publicly acknowledged. The feminine role was one of support, an appendage who provided silent companionship. Fathers of the middle and upper classes usually regarded the education of their daughters as an unnecessary expense. The working class father sent his daughter to a mill or a factory as swiftly as possible in the need to augment the household income. There were few girls' schools of note and until the late 1840s, there was no higher education for women. This era is now considered to be the heyday of natural science, a time when ladies, gentlemen and indeed whole families were gripped by the fervour of exploring the out-of-doors. Yet, one must not forget that this was also a time of slavery and industrialisation which brought with it child labour in mines, factories and mills. Victorian society was divided. However, it was also a period of social reform and change, both social and intellectual.

Charles Kingsley writes in *Glaucus, or The Wonders of the Shore*: 'I have seen the young London beauty, amid all the excitement and temptation of luxury and flattery, with her heart pure and her mind occupied in a boudoir full of shells and fossils, flowers and seaweeds…' Sadly, illustrations aside, little of the research undertaken by women made its way into print. This was in spite of the availability of cheaper books, a direct result of the 1861 repeal of a taxation on newspapers, pamphlets and paper. This tax had been introduced in the reign of Queen Anne to raise revenue for war, but in all probability it was also intended to curb the publication of revolutionary ideas in the popular press.

Victorian beachcombing trips took place in an era of female delicacy. It was hoped that the 'sea air' might provide a convalescent atmosphere, and if seaweeding provoked reading of natural history it was deemed for amusement, not research. The Channel Isles author Louisa Lane Clarke notes this in the introduction to her little book, *Common Seaweeds of the British Coast and Channel Islands* (1865):

> *There is felt by many seaside ramblers to be a want of some unscientific, easy Guide to the Seaweeds and contents of rock-pools on the English coast. There are most valuable works by HARVEY and LANDSBOROUGH on the subject, but more*

expensive and more scientific than suits the minds of those who seek for health and rest in the sweet summer months by the seaside.

Elizabeth Anne Allom, the author of *The Sea-Weed Collector* (1841) was also mindful of the healthy aspect of seaweeding: '[T]he most scrupulously delicate lady may walk with comfort along the beautifully level sands and collect the most interesting specimens of marine vegetation without the slightest danger or inconvenience from damp or cold.'

MARGARET GATTY (1809–73)

Margaret Gatty, who also published under the name Mrs Alfred Gatty, was a naturalist, correspondent and seaweed expert. She edited the periodical *Aunt Judy's Magazine*, and wrote eighteen children's books – notably, *Parables from Nature* (1857), *The Book of Emblems* (1872), *The Book of Sun-Dials* (1872), and the popular scientific text, *British Sea-Weeds* (1863 and 1872). She also, with her family, helped to compile the autobiography of the Jewish Missionary, Dr Joseph Wolff. Charles Kingsley, who was at the time Regis Professor of History at Cambridge, praised Gatty's 'masculine' powers of research. Gatty was nevertheless irritated by Kingsley's review of *British Sea-Weeds*, perhaps because it lavishly praised the colour illustrations, which were taken from Dr Harvey's *Phycologia Britannica*. Gatty was an amateur but with a keenness for scholarly learning. She certainly appears to have been held in high esteem by other seaweed writers of her time.

In 1839, Margaret married the Reverend Alfred Gatty, who had a living in Ecclesfield, South Yorkshire. After the birth of her seventh child Undine at the age of thirty-nine, Gatty became bronchial – the burdens of parish life and motherhood had taken their toll, and on 14 December 1848, accompanied by her eldest son Reginald, she was sent to convalesce in Hastings on the South coast. The Gattys kept a confession book at Ecclesfield,

Margaret Gatty (1809–73).

and Margaret's plea was to live somewhere warm by the sea. From December 1848 to July 1849 her wish was granted. Whilst recuperating, Gatty made the acquaintance of a local doctor who interested her in seaweeds. He lent her a copy of William Harvey's *Phycologia Britannica*. Gatty collected seaweeds with gusto and discovered a love of seaweeding that would stay with her for life. Her talent for observation is seen from a diary comment: 'All the pictures of *Delesseria sanguinea* are the colour it fades to rather than the clear delicate brown it has when freshly gathered.' Gatty's meticulous shore side observation was of benefit to male academics sitting in the warmth of their university studies. She collected seaweeds whenever it was possible (not an easy pastime as a resident of landlocked Ecclesfield), and encouraged her family and friends to do likewise. In the census of 1851 she is described as a 'Clergyman's wife, Algologist'. It seems natural therefore that Gatty developed a correspondence with an authority on zoophytes and seaweed, Dr George Johnston of Berwick on Tweed, one of the founders of the Berwickshire Naturalists' Club. During the years following her father's death in 1855, Gatty sought solace in Johnston's company on seaweed expeditions. She showed her gratitude to him in a dedication in her children's book *Parables from Nature*. There was also correspondence with George Busk, an expert on bryozoans, a type of marine invertebrate similar to coral. He would subsequenty name several new species after Gatty. Over this ten-year period she also wrote to Dr Harvey (the author whose seaweed book she had been lent in Hastings). Over time, Gatty acted as a buffer, dealing with correspondence sent to Harvey by less able scholars. Indeed, there is evidence that the intimacy of the writers worried both parties (they eventually met in 1860), but the letters ceased with Harvey's death in May 1866.

In 1857 she wrote to Dr Harvey: 'I have long contemplated making an attempt at a Horn Book of Algology [a 'hornbook' was an educational primer]. I do not see that Dr Landsborough's *Popular Seaweeds* has in reality simplified the study.' Gatty had written in other genres, but now she was off to the seaside. Note her use of the word simplified – she wrote at a time when women did not merit a university education.

The introduction to Gatty's *British Sea-Weeds* makes delightful reading and its enthusiasm for seaweeding is infectious. Gatty's understanding of marine science is evident throughout the text, such as where she describes seaweed zonation:

On leaving the Laminarian zone of Filey Bridge you have the opportunity, rarely afforded by one mass of rocks, of ascending gradually by a succession of, for the most part, square-cut levels, or ledges, each easy to walk upon, and abounding in pools, up to extreme high-water mark on the top; one part of which is only completely submerged at spring-tides, though always within the influence of spray. And here, as you walk over the fine old riddled surface, nearly a quarter of a mile in extent, you have but to turn to the right hand, where some large blocks of stone rise up in a sloping position, and underneath the slope you may gather handfuls of Catenella opuntia, as you stand; while in the adjoining pools the grass-green Enteromorphas come, obedient to the zone law which gives them the upper level as their peculiar habitat.

In her meticulously prepared seaweed text, which took fourteen years of research to complete, she comments on almost two hundred species in a simple yet thoughtful way, placing emphasis on the importance of classification. However, she consistently acknowledged herself as a self-taught amateur, recommending phycology as an appropriate pastime for those interested in learning about the goodness of God.

Gatty's *British Sea-Weeds* was published in two volumes in 1872, the year before she died. The Revd Landsborough may have popularised seaweed, but Gatty's two-volume publication was the more substantial.

ELLEN HUTCHINS (1785–1815)

Ellen Hutchins, heralded as Ireland's first female botanist, described seaweeds as 'a curious and difficult branch' of botany. Her interest is known as cryptogrammic botany – the study of non-flowering plants in which reproduction is by spores, not flowers or seeds. Hutchins appreciated the intricate detail of lichen, mosses and seaweeds and realised that beauty need not necessarily be scented or floral.

Like many females of her era, Hutchins produced exquisite seaweed illustrations. She benefited from the encouragement of her physician Dr Stokes, Professor of Medicine at the Royal College of Surgeons, who advised her to lead an open-air life. Stokes, a keen bryologist (bryology being the study of mosses), also lectured in natural history and endorsed outdoor exploration for its health benefits. He introduced Hutchins to James Townsend Mackay (1775–1862), the founder and curator of the Botanic Garden at Trinity College, who also assisted her education hugely. It was while on a visit to Ballylickey in 1805 that Mackay advised Hutchins to take up the study of seaweeds.

In 1807, Mackay sent Hutchins's specimens to the Great Yarmouth-based botanist Dawson Turner (1875–1858), who used Hutchins' Irish illustrations for his seaweed publication, *Historia*

Fucorum (1807). Turner's thank you note to Hutchins triggered a seven-year correspondence and an exchange of specimens that continued until her early death at the age of twenty-nine. Her first letter concentrated on one of the *codium* species, velvet horn (*Fucus tomentosus*): 'Dear Sir, Your most interesting letter found me employed finishing the drawing you wished for of *Fucus tomentosus*. I have sent it with drawings of some *Confervae*… These are the very first that I have attempted.' She continued: 'I had great pleasure in finding *Fucus tomentosus* in fruit…fearing that drying will alter its appearance, I have attempted to draw it as it appeared when recent.'

Hutchins's letter shows her attention to detail, noting the colour change as seaweeds dries. When writing *Flora Hibernica* (1836), Mackay included many of Ellen's specimens. Indeed, the first time that seaweeds were classified by their biochemical character (pigments – colour) was in this publication. MacKay wrote the book in partnership with William Harvey. Hutchins bequeathed her illustrated collection to Dawson Turner, but it was later given to his son-in-law, Sir William Hooker. Some of the illustrations were subsequently passed by Hooker to William Harvey, who in turn gave drawings to Margaret Gatty. After Margaret Gatty's death, Hutchins' drawings were donated by Gatty's daughter to Sheffield Museum.

Anne Elizabeth Ball (1808–72)

Anne Elizabeth Ball from County Cork was another important Irish algologist. Professor Mike Guiry concedes that she is not as well remembered as Hutchins because, like him, she was born in Youghal, which Guiry describes as a miserable beach for algae because it is sandy. Anne Ball simply did not have as many opportunities for collecting specimens in Youghal as Miss Hutchins in Bantry Bay. Seaweeds require a rocky shore. Ball would have little chance to go rock pooling. Anne's brother, Robert Ball, was director of the museum of Trinity College,

Dublin, from 1844 until his death in 1857. The siblings collected algae for Harvey. In a letter to Robert, dated 24 May 1834, about a forthcoming research trip to Ireland, Harvey advised him to take 'some bibulous paper, some white and some boards, and gather algae at Aran'. Harvey rejoiced to hear that Anne had taken an interest in collecting seaweed: 'Urge her to work hard this summer,' he told her brother, 'for I want some new things for Mackay's *Flora*'.

Anne Ball's records were included in Mackay's *Flora Hibernica*. and Harvey dedicated the genus *Ballia*, a red seaweed from Australia, to her. She discovered the rare *Sporochnus cabrera* and is commemorated by the seaweed she discovered, *Cladophora balliana*. The seaweed *B. Robertiana* was named posthumously in honour of her brother.

Amelia Warren Griffiths (1768–1858)

When Margaret Gatty was eight years old, the reputation of another seaweeder, Amelia Griffiths, was already renowned. Mrs Griffiths's seaweed fame was extensive. William Harvey held her work in high esteem and relied upon her collecting expertise for his encyclopaedic phycology book. He dedicated the 1849 edition of *A Manual of the British Marine Algae* to her: 'If I lean to glorify any one, it is Mrs Griffiths, to whom I owe much of the little acquaintance I have with the variations to which these plants are subject, and who is always ready to supply me with fruits of plants which every one else finds barren. She is worth ten thousand other collectors.' On one occasion Dr Harvey visited Mrs Griffiths and noted that she was seventy-six years of age and that they'd gathered *Gigartina teedii* together in its only British habitat – the same spot where Mrs Griffiths had made its discovery in 1811, the year of Harvey's birth.

Amelia Griffiths was instructed in seaweeding by the Revd Samuel Goodenough (1743–1819) who, along with James Edward

Smith (1743–1827) and Thomas Marsham (1748–1819), was a founder member of the Linnaean Society of London.

In 1808, Dawson Turner acknowledged Griffiths's 'unwearied zeal and extraordinary acuteness'. Unsurprisingly, therefore, Griffiths's discovery of a holotype genus was eponymously named *Griffithsia* by the Swedish botanist Carl Adolph Agardh in 1817. Griffiths, in partnership with Mary Wyatt, her former servant who now kept a shell shop in Torquay, produced two volumes of pressed Devonshire seaweeds. These books were published in 1833 under the title *Algae Danmoniensis*. Each volume contained fifty different species from the Devon and Cornish coast. The numbered specimens were named (in Latin), referenced to Dr Hooker's *British Flora* and included a note of the substrate where each specimen was found, its location and its rarity.

Interestingly, it is the name of Griffiths's former servant that features on the title page, which states that the book was 'Prepared and Sold by Mary Wyatt, Dealer in Shells'. Between 1833 and 1836 Wyatt went on to produce volumes three and four of *Algae Danmonienses*. A royal dedication to the Duchess of Kent and Princess Victoria may have enhanced the book's sales.

Griffiths was a vicar's widow with five children, but she was financially secure enough to enjoy seaweeding. V.J. Chapman writes that Camille Sauvageau, a French marine botanist, suggested that Mrs Griffiths pickled *Gracilaria compressa* (now *Gracilaria bursapastoris*). The *Gracilaria* species produce agar not carrageenan, and it would seem to me a funny species for Mrs Griffiths to be pickling. However, whether this culinary information is reliable or not, Griffiths gave generously of both her knowledge and her specimens.

When Griffiths began her seaweed forays, identification of species was difficult as many had not been named or described clearly, so in common with many others of her era she devised her own names – 'bottle brush' being one such name. Another vicar's wife, Louisa Lane Clarke, writes of the aptly-named

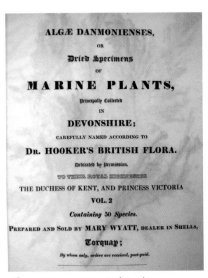

ALGÆ DANMONIENSES,

OR

Dried Specimens

OF

MARINE PLANTS,

Principally Collected

IN

DEVONSHIRE;

CAREFULLY NAMED ACCORDING TO

DR. HOOKER'S BRITISH FLORA.

Dedicated by Permission.

TO THEIR ROYAL HIGHNESSES

THE DUCHESS OF KENT, AND PRINCESS VICTORIA

VOL. 2

Containing 50 Species.

PREPARED AND SOLD BY MARY WYATT, DEALER IN SHELLS,

Torquay;

By whom only, orders are received, post-paid.

Algae Danmoniensis (1833)

seaweed peacocks tail (*Padina pavonica*): 'Many authors have compared this admired seaweed to the expanded tail of the peacock, and probably thence it derives its name; truly, the play of colour on the frond beneath the water is so beautiful, we bend to gaze upon it, and forget to gather it.'

Collecting seaweeds was an acceptable female activity and grappling with untamed nature offered a deeper understanding of God's creation. Beaches were scavenged for pretty specimens, which were taken home and pressed artistically, or displayed in marine aquaria. It was a convivial recreation and an ideal way to pass time at the seaside. Cambridge academic Dr Anne Secord notes in a paper on the work of Amelia Warren Griffiths: 'Griffiths maintained an interest in marine botany up to her death in 1858, by which date the increasing enthusiasm for seaside studies had tipped seaweed collecting into a fashionable craze.' Secord continues: 'On the more serious end of the scale, Victorian seaweed collectors like Margaret Gatty, are noted as some of the least hidden of women contributors to science.' In her 'Recollections of Ilfracombe' the novelist George Eliot (Mary Ann Evans) contemplates the way in which identifying species of seaweed helped her to make sense of the world. Eliot was in all probability encouraged by her partner, the philosopher and critic George Henry Lewes, who was also the author of *Sea-Side Studies at Ilfracombe, Tenby, The Scilly Isles, and Jersey* (1860).

ANNE PRATT (1806–1893)

Anne Pratt connected with seaweed through her delicate health, which led to her becoming a prolific reader. She writes that Dr Cullen used to say that he had cured weak stomachs by engaging his patients in the study of botany.

Self taught, she was published through her Christian contacts – the Religious Tract Society and the Society for Promoting Christian Knowledge. The SPCK published her book, *Chapters on the Common Things of the Sea-Coast* in 1850. Chapter Two is on seaweeds, and in common with other ladies interested in benthic studies, Pratt stated that the use of scientific terms would be out of place in her book. After a brief digression into botanical poetry and cooking seaweed, she wrote: 'The Sweet Laminaria [sugar kelp] is eaten, boiled, when in a young state, but it can be the food of those only who are almost destitute of any other provision, for it is neither palatable nor nutritious, though valuable for manure, and for the kelp it affords.' Hardly encouragement for using seaweed as an ingredient. However, Pratt went on to say that in Japan seaweed was used for several purposes – sometimes for food ('It is cut into pieces, which by boiling become much thickened, and it is then taken with food'), and sometimes as a kind of ceremonial decoration affixed to paper to accompany gifts. She also quoted Sir William Hooker's observations on dulse:

> *On the Scotch coast, it is eaten raw by the natives, and in the county of Caithness, in particular, I have seen a number of women and children gathering it from the rocks and devouring it with great avidity.*

However, she conceded that dulse was not a peasant food and wrote that 'many who can afford to procure costly food relish it still, perhaps because it brings with it some associations of childhood, as some of us may now like the blackberries or other wild fruits, because they remind us of by-gone times, and happy hours in the woodlands'. Pratt wrote that dulse had 'an odour of violets' and was eaten before breakfast because 'of its properties in cleansing the blood'. Pratt also recommended cooking carrageen. As a Christian, her philanthropic hope was that 'a small portion of meat, accompanied by a good quantity of the carrageen moss, well boiled, would furnish a wholesome meal to many a poor family, who, at the same expense, could procure only a much less nourishing diet'. In common with Isabella Gifford and Louisa Lane Clarke she speaks of 'tribes' of seaweeds (not groups), mentioning that the *Laminaria* tribe have been well called the giants of the marine flora.

ELIZABETH ANNE ALLOM (FL. 1840S–1870)

Elizabeth Allom, the daughter of the Revd S.R. Allom, illustrated her book *The Sea-Weed Collector* (1841) with thirty-six natural specimens gathered from the shores of Margate and Ramsgate.

Allom also wrote poetry (rather macabrely, *Death Scenes and Other Poems*, 1844), and a lovely children's story titled *Sea-side Pleasures, or a Peep at Miss Eldon's Happy Pupils* (1845). This latter is a delightful educational tale about a holiday in Ramsgate taken by a London-based family. Ellen aged fourteen is educated about seaweeds by her governess: 'The algae, or sea weeds, together with grasses, lichens and mosses, form, as I dare say you will recollect, the lowest order of botany, cryptogamia.' We hear that Ellen is equipped with an oilskin-lined basket for seaweed collecting, and a portfolio in which to arrange the seaweeds when dry. The teenager is described as an algologist (which has now been replaced by the word phycologist) or collector of marine or sea plants. In the story, seaweeds are described in detail as Ellen collects and later teaches her mother about them. One of her favourites is *Delesseria sanguinea*: 'I think, mama, its colour is as bright and clear as that of your favourite rose; and see the delicate branching veins, making it look like a red palm-leaf or a crimson feather!' Her mother replies: 'It is indeed, my love, a most exquisite specimen of the skill of the great Creator.' Allom placed God at the centre of her writing, rejoicing in creation as a spiritual act.

FORAGING FOR SEAWEED

These British female authors encouraged Victorians to forage, identify and record nature's plants. Stephen E. Hunt, writing about women's love of seaweed, describes this as mid-Victorian biophilia (the human connection with nature). During the 1850s, exploration of the coast was aided by greater ease of access brought about by the expansion of the railway network. The availability of affordable microscopes was also pertinent to those who wanted to explore the finer structure of seaweed. A twelve-year-old Margaret Gatty was fortunate to be left her maternal grandmother's Culpeper tripod microscope (now housed in Sheffield Industrial Museums), which was useful for her seaweed studies. In her introduction to *British Sea-Weeds* (Volume 1) Mrs Gatty included a brief account entitled 'How to Make Sections of Algae For Microscopic Examination'.

Queen Victoria was known to favour seaweeding, and indeed Prince Albert

Advertisement for M Smout, seaweed florist.

was keen for his children to familiarise themselves with nature. Thanks to influence and serendipity, via a lady-in-waiting to Queen Victoria, Mrs Gatty obliged Prince Albert by sending his children a seaweed book (which was presented on 30 June 1854). Mrs Gatty was, like many ladies of her era, keen to use her books in a philanthropic capacity. Indeed, small subscriptions from *Aunt Judy's Magazine* were given towards cot beds for the Hospital for Sick Children in Great Ormond Street. The 'Cot List', the first sponsored beds for children in any hospital, became a prominent feature in the magazine. The funds would appear to have been segregated for cots for boys and girls, but as school playgrounds were also separated along similar lines this was not unusual for the time.

Seaweed was in vogue. It had style and tangled its way into Victorian needlework, collages and even Staffordshire china. In 1883, Josiah Wedgwood entered the seaweed craze with the production of a brown, marine flora design. William Kilburn (1745-1818), a designer of English calico, captured the novelty of untamed seaweeds in his fabrics. An 1832 testimonial to Kilburn claims that 'his pieces of muslin chintzes sold for a guinea a yard, and he had the honour of presenting one of them, the seaweed pattern, designed by himself, to her majesty Queen Charlotte'.

The collections of Queen Charlotte (1774-1818) and the Duchess of Portland (1715-85) both contained pressed seaweed specimens. The mysterious beauty of seaweeds sets them apart from the more flamboyant, easily recognisable flowering plants. M. & C.L. Smout owned a seaweed florist shop in Hastings in 1890 and suggested to customers that seaweeds rivalled flowers in their varied beauty. The Smouts' sales pitch enthused about using seaweeds for dress trimmings, table decorations, drawing room ornaments and even yacht decoration. The provenance of their seaweed was assured in a way that we champion local food today. Sadly, it would appear that seaweed peaked around the late 1890s, and the Smouts' seaweed shop was given notice in the *London Gazette* (31 March 1892) by the official receiver, Cecil Mercer.

The late eighteenth and nineteenth century seaweed collectors were predated by a vogue for fine furniture embossed with 'seaweed marquetry' (patterns resembling seaweed). Sadly, its popularity was short-lived, perhaps a contemporary cabinet maker will reconsider the idea. In more recent years, Michael Silver combined his talent for photography and his work as a chef in the production of a series of prints which included sheets of nori. Seaweed as art continues to be fashionable in the new millennium. Josie Iselin, a talented San Francisco-based artist, works with imagination to demonstrate just how stunning seaweed is. In the UK, seaweed prints are available from Argyll artist, Charlotte Goodlet. Both Iselin and Goodlet capture the beauty of seaweed through nature-inspired art. The ocean's flowers are varied and exquisitely beautiful.

COLLECTING SEAWEED

Mrs Gatty acknowledged the help of Miss Catherine Cutler for a roly-poly towel method of drying and carrying seaweeds. In a chapter entitled 'Rules For Preserving And Laying Out Sea-Weeds', she wrote: 'It is to a well-known algologist, my friend Miss Cutler, that I am indebted for these hints, and as the plan was practised by her in my behalf on the occasion of a hurried visit to the shore of Exmouth, and many of the plants were laid out successfully the following day, I have no hesitation in recommending it in cases of inevitable hurry.' To each species of seaweed there was a method, and she concluded with: 'Now for a few words upon special plants. The "tough leathery" olive ones, *Sargassum, Cystoseira, Fucus &c*, should be soaked for an hour or two in hot water before being laid out and pressed, as they are thereby rendered more pliable.'

Margaret Gatty enjoyed several seaweeding expeditions with Miss Cutler, and after the helpful Devon-based collector died in 1866, was sent some of her seaweed specimens. These are included in Gatty's personal seaweed collection, which is now housed in the St

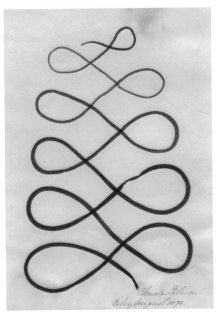

Chorda filum, collected by Margaret Gatty, in Filey, Yorkshire, 1871. MG0079 in the Margaret Gatty herbarium, STA.

Andrews Herbarium. This collection of seaweeds was given to the Gatty Marine Laboratory at St Andrews by Gatty's daughter, Horatia Katherine Eden, in April 1907. It includes more than 8,825 specimens which the STA is reorganising – a challenging task. Both Gatty and Cutler had seaweeds named in their honour. *Cutleria* is a brown seaweed named after Catherine Cutler by Dr Robert Kaye Greville who described Miss Cutler as 'a most acute and zealous algologist and the discoverer of *Grateloupia filicina*'. Hutchins, Griffiths and Gatty had seaweeds named in their honour too. I am indebted to Professor Mike Guiry for sending me the following not insignificant list of seaweeds named after women:

Margaret Gatty:
Gattya Harvey
Carpococcus gattyae J. Agardh,
Cladophora gattyae Harvey
Nitophyllum gattyanum J. Agardh

Amelia Warren Griffiths:
Griffithsia C. Agardh
Gymnogongrus griffithsiae (Turner) Martius
Stictyosiphon griffithsianus Holmes & Batters

Catherine Cutler:
Cutleria Greville
Grateloupia cutleriae Kützing

Ellen Hutchins:
Hutchinsia C. Agardh. This was named in her honour by Carl Adolph Agardh professor of botany at Lund, but unfortunately, the (alpine) flowering plant genus *Hutchinsia* (*Brassicaceae*) had been named previously by Robert Brown, so *Hutchinsia* the alga was not used thereafter.

SEAWEEDING ATTIRE

Margaret Gatty enjoyed her activities collecting seaweed alfresco and her experiences may have helped to change attitudes regarding Victorian clothing, encouraging a loosening of the usual formal dress codes of the era. This sartorial advice is taken from Volume 1 of Gatty's *British Sea-Weeds* – what a picture to behold, hats full of seaweed and petticoats hitched above the knee:

About this shore-hunting, however, as regards my own sex (so many of whom, I know, are interested in the pursuit), many difficulties are apt to arise; among the foremost of which must be mentioned the risk of cold and destruction of clothes. The best pair of single-soled kid Balmoral boots that ever were made will not stand salt water many days – indeed would scarcely 'come on' after being thoroughly wetted two or three times in succession – and the sea-weed collector who has to pick her way to save her boots will never be a loving disciple as long as she lives! Any one, therefore, really intending to work in the matter, must lay aside for a time all thought of conventional appearances, and be content to support the weight of a pair of boy's shooting boots, which, furthermore, should be rendered as far water-proof as possible by receiving a thin coat of neat's foot oil, such as is used by fishermen…

Next to boots comes the question of petticoats; and if anything could excuse a woman for imitating the costume of a man, it would be what she suffers as a sea-weed collector from those necessary draperies! But to make the best of a bad matter, let woollen be in the ascendant as much as possible; and let the petticoats never come below the ankle. A ladies' yatching [sic] costume has come into fashion of late, which is, perhaps, as near perfection for shore-work as anything that could be devised. It is a suit consisting of a full short skirt of blue flannel or serge (like very fine bathing-gown material), with waistcoat and jacket to match. Cloaks and shawls, which necessarily hamper the arms, besides having long ends and corners which cannot fail to get soaked, are, of course, very inconvenient, and should be as much avoided as possible.…In conclusion, a hat is preferable to a bonnet, merino stockings to cotton ones, and a strong pair of gloves is indispensable. All millinery work – silks, satins, lace, bracelets, and other jewellery, &c. must, and will, be laid aside by every rational being who attempts to shore-hunt.

Louisa Lane Clarke endorsed Gatty's casual attire in her book *Common Seaweeds of the British Coast and Channel Islands*: 'We are going for seaweeds. The tin can is slung over one shoulder, an oilskin bag is at our girdle for smaller and more precious specimens, a pole to steady our feet, with a hook at one end to lift the tangled masses of rough weed away.'

FAMILY SEAWEEDING

Gatty was avant garde, a woman ahead of her time. Her friend, the algologist Dr George Johnston, first introduced Gatty to chloroform, which she described as 'Angel's Food'. Chloroform was looked upon with some suspicion in England, but not so in Scotland, where Johnston maintained it was administered more satisfactorily. Margaret Gatty was the first mother in Sheffield to be administered chloroform for pain relief during the birth of her ninth child, Charles, in 1851. Over the years, Gatty travelled extensively within the British Isles to source her seaweed specimens. This would have incurred travel expenses and required a supportive spouse. Her husband Alfred, an author in his own right, negotiated her publishing contracts and marketed her books, as well as – we must assume – earning his stipend. The children who were taken to the seaside unsurprisingly had a keen interest in marine algae too, and they also wrote short stories. An entry in Gatty's diary from 1850 records: 'Set off for Filey, Alfred, self, seven children, two nurses and the cook. Arrived safely. D.G. [her daughter, Dot Gatty] went down to the sand and found seaweeds.' Staff helped Gatty in the home, and in all probability on the seashore too.

The chief Gatty child enthusiast was her third daughter, Horatia Katherine Frances, commonly known as Dot. By the time Dot was eight years old she was considered an authority on 'seaweedising', as the children called their mother's obsession. Juliana noted in her diary on 15 December 1861, when Dot was fifteen: 'Tea in the drawing room. Afterwards Dot & Mother retired to seaweedise.'

The Gatty boys were sent to public school, but the girls were educated in the home until their teens. In their love of seaweed, Victorian algologists found an interest that went far beyond a pastime. It enabled them to enjoy the sea air, and many, like Gatty, extended this invitation to family and friends. Mothers encouraged an interest in natural history at a time when schools took little interest. From the mid-century onwards a large number of natural history books were published for children.

The Gatty children certainly found themselves knee-deep in seaweed and seaweed correspondence. In 1856 the family went to the Isle of Man, and their mother wrote: 'Every seaweed had to be laid out in our bedroom, in which during the last fortnight, Dot also slept in a little bed. How we managed our pans and dishes and the drying of muslins and blotting papers and the clearing away of messes as to leave the room sweet and habitable, I leave you to judge! Viewed at a distance I should say the timing was impossible; but by a never-ending vigilance and labour in one direction, the seaweeds were washed, cleaned, laid out and dried, and here they are.' If you thought that life in a Victorian vicarage was straight-laced and dull, you may have to think again.

ANNA ATKINS

John Children, father of the botanist and photographer Anna Atkins (1799-1871), was a scientist and secretary of the Royal Entomological Society. The father and daughter relationship became close after the death of Anna's mother, Hester, in 1800. John Children nurtured his daughter's interest in botany, natural science and early photography. They collaborated to provide hand-drawn illustrations for the translation of Jean-Baptist Lamarck's *Genera of Shells* (1799, translated 1823). However, John Children's contacts helped too. In February 1839 he was present at a Royal Society meeting at which a Wiltshire landowner, William Henry Fox Talbot, outlined his exciting new invention: the creation of 'photograms'. This used chemicals and sunlight to create images on paper, and led to the development of camera-made images. Anna's father wrote to Talbot telling him: 'My daughter and I shall set to work in good earnest 'till we completely succeed in practising your invaluable process.' At the same time as William Harvey was being helped by Amelia Warren Griffiths and Margaret Gatty, Anna Atkins began recording British seaweeds. Atkins did this not by pressing her specimens between blotting paper, but by using Herschel's photographic technique of 'blueprinting' or cyanotyping. Seaweed was pressed, under glass, on paper that had been sensitised with a mixture of soluble iron salts, and then exposed to the sun. After washing in water, the background colour deepened to a celestial blue, leaving the detailed outline of the algae in grey. This was then washed and dried to fix the colour and the image.

The first issue of *Photographs of British Algae: Cyanotype Impressions* was published (privately) in October 1843 under the pseudonym 'A.A'. Subsequent parts were issued over the next ten years. Each contained around 400 images. It is not known how many copies Atkins made, but fewer than twenty still survive, all are slightly different. As an exemplary amateur, Atkins expected no income from *British Algae*. Her botanical interest was for her own edification. Atkins' father acted as mediator first with introductions, and then by giving her work to prominent members of the scientific community. Anna Atkins is considered the first female photographer and *Photographs of British Algae,* the first photographed book of seaweed. It is a stunning example of natural history imagery. Unlike Wyatt's *Algae Danmonienses,* which is bulky, Atkin's *Britsh Algae* is a slim volume of life-sized images. It highlights the beauty of ocean flowers, while at the same time being a useful reference for identification.

Anna Thynne

James Shirley Hibberd (1825-90) was a Victorian writer and horticulturalist. In his book, *Rustic Adornments for Homes of Taste* (1870), he describes where and how to collect seaweeds, and how to build an aquarium. However, the first London marine aquarium is accredited to Anna Thynne, wife of the Reverend Lord John Thynne, sub-dean of Westminster Abbey. Prior to building her first aquarium in 1846, Anna appears to have involved her servants in the more monotonous jobs involved in trying to keep marine specimens alive in salt water. Returning from Torquay to London, for example, Anna would bring back stone corals and put them in her cook's collection of pie dishes, which the servants were tasked with filling with salt water, which had to be emptied and refreshed on a daily basis. Suffice to say, the pie dishes proved inadequate, and so the aquarium was invented. With the help of her naturalist friend, Philip Henry Gosse, Anna popularised glass 'theatres', and ushered in a period of 'aquarium mania', and therein the study of marine life in its natural state.

INTERACTION WITH MEN: HUSBANDS & ACADEMICS

In *British Sea-Weeds*, Mrs Gatty acknowledged that 'men certainly have an advantage over women, for they can wade with impunity'. But men sometimes had their advantages:

> *...with a male companion to lend a hand and infuse a sense of security, a very* eerie *hunting-ground may sometimes be ventured upon...[I]n reflecting upon the best and easiest shores, such as the choice one of Douglas Bay, Isle of Man, for instance, it must be owned that a low-water-mark expedition is more comfortably undertaken under the protection of a gentleman'. He may fossilize, sketch, or (if he* will *be savage and barbaric) shoot gulls...*

The presence of a man, however, was not a prerequisite for correctly identifying marine algae, and there was 'no need to involve him in the messing after what he may consider 'rubbish', unless, happily, he is inclined to assist'.

In spite of what Gatty calls 'the sisterhood' being diffident and self-effacing, seaweed provided a new sphere for women within botany. Gatty refused to push herself forward as an authoritative voice, but such modesty was indicative of females of her era. However, she was not pleased when she made mistakes, and blamed them on her lack of a formal education.

The illustrative help given by Emily Bowes Gosse to her husband Henry's work remains largely unacknowledged, a mark of the silent companionship of the Victorian wife.

However, the very fact that some seaweed species are named after female pioneers in the field at least acknowledges a level of appreciation. Women were not invited to become members of the Linnaean Society until 1919, so for many years taxonomy remained a male domain. It should however, be noted that both Robert Kaye Greville and David Landsborough rated female seaweed collectors highly. Landsborough, in his book *A Popular History of British Sea-Weeds*, cites seven female and six male algologists among the extensive acknowledgements in the preface to his 1851 edition. For Landsborough, Amelia Griffiths was the *facile Regina* – the 'Queen of Algologists'. Griffiths had, as Stephen E. Hunt points out, 'set a precedent as an outstanding authority in this area'. Despite discovering several species during the 1830s and 1840s, Griffiths did not make her work public – at least through the usual channels of publishing. As Landsborough goes on to explain, Griffiths 'published nothing in her own name', nevertheless 'she may yet be said to have published much, as she has so often been consulted by distinguished naturalists, who have been proud to acknowledge the benefit they have derived from her scientific eye and sound judgment'.

Although women were not considered scientists, a handful earned unprecedented recognition in what was at that point a male-dominated profession. The seaweed sisterhood raised awareness of the diversity of marine plants, and their stages of growth and reproduction from 'infancy to decay'. Many ladies noted seasonal variation. But it was not just in the UK that nineteenth century female seaweed collectors contributed to projects. Dr Harvey dedicated each volume of *Phycologia Australica* to collectors he respected, and noted with regard to Australian algae: 'This species is named in compliment to Mrs Fereday, of Georgetown, in whose collection I first saw some fine specimens. Subsequently I collected it in considerable plenty in the Tamar, above Georgetown, where it is occasionally drifted ashore in large quantity.'

SEAWEEDING FOR WELLBEING

Seaweed provided a means for the comfortably off, middle-class Victorian lady to relieve a dull domestic routine. A sense of danger, perhaps, heightened the natural attraction of the seaside. Beyond the vagaries of the weather, seaweeders were at the mercy of the ebb and flow of the tide. Victorian ladies were taught to draw and were avid collectors, so it is not surprising that their seaweed illustrations were exact and extensive. It was also an opportunity to engage in intellectual company. The collection of seaweed provided an excellent compromise between personal aspirations and conventional Victorian female behaviour. An amateur seaweed collage may be seen as simply a piece of beautiful craftwork, but when catalogued, mounted and published in a book, it also demonstrated precision and accuracy.

Seaweeding was a revitalising activity, both mentally and physically, for the algologist. Mrs Gatty's convalescent beachcombing could be compared to a twenty-first century course of antidepressants. Writing to her sister-in-law, she advised her: 'Have your microscope out when you can…Or take advantage of odd times. I am very sure if you once get into the pursuit [of seaweed collecting] you will find it next to meat drink & clothing! I mean your seaweed hours will be a sort of necessary repast to you.'

In *The Wonders of the Shore*, intended to be an introduction to natural history for children, Charles Kingsley wrote of the positive effect outdoor activities such as the study of seaweed could have on the feelings and the intellect: 'Those who have followed it [the study of natural history], especially on the sea-shore…can tell from experience, that over and above its accessory charms of pure sea-breezes, and wild rambles by cliff and loch, the study itself has had a weighty moral effect upon their hearts and spirits.' By contrast, Gatty placed less emphasis on the morally beneficial aspect of seaweeding, and her description of how she experienced the sea shore has a more exuberant, liberating feel to it: '[T]o walk where you are walking makes you feel free, bold and joyous, monarch of all you survey, untrammelled, at ease, at home! At home, though among all manner of strange, unknown creatures, flung at your feet every minute by the quick succeeding waves.'

AMERICAN SEA-WEEDERS.

Mary Brewster of Bristol, Connecticut, is often cited as America's Margaret Gatty. Brewster's birthday greetings to the poet Henry Wadsworth Longfellow, included twelve seaweed specimens that she had meticulously collected and pressed.

A pioneering American academic with an interest in seaweed was Professor Josephine Tilden, of the landlocked University of Minnesota. Tilden was its first female scientist and specialised in phycology, despite the logistical problems that geography often imposed on the study of seaweed. In 1898, for example, during one seaweed-hunting expedition, she travelled by canoe over the Strait of Juan de Fuca with her sixty-year-old mother as a chaperone. It was here, at Port Renfrew on the west coast of Vancouver Island, that Tilden would establish the Minnesota Seaside Station, with the aim of studying its seaweed. As she remembered it many years later:

> *The algae covering that exposed shore were beyond my wildest dreams. I spent every daylight moment in collecting algae. At stated intervals my mother doled out warmed up beans and tea. At the end of the fourth day, Mr Baird (the landowner) said to me, 'I am going to give you a deed for the best four acres on my place. Take your choice.' I chose, and that spot became the site of the Minnesota Seaside Station.*

Writing in *Scientific America* in 1928, in an essay prophetically titled, 'Down to the Sea, for Seaweed may be the Next Step in

Replacing Our Disappearing Sources of Food Supplies', Tilden noted that seaweed was a rich source of vitamins: 'Since marine algae are even richer in these food-factors than are marine animals, they too should be added to our food. Powdered seaweeds when mixed in small amounts with other food cannot be tasted. In larger amounts they impart a pleasing taste and are much relished by persons accustomed to their use.' The pluck and determination of this avant garde seaweed enthusiast is admirable. Although Professor Tilden's scientific station was abandoned in 1906, her work and that of her students was published in *Postelsia: the Year Book of the Minnesota Seaside Station*, and in six volumes devoted to dried algae, issued under the title *American Algae* (1894–1902).

THE PRESENT DAY

A list of more contemporary female phycolgists would include the Scottish algologist Dorothy Constance Gibb (1907–2006), who won the Dickie Prize in Botany at Aberdeen University, Lily Newton (1893-81), Elsie Conway (1902-92), Mary Parke (1908-89) and Elsie Burrows. Not to mention Professor Juliet Brodie of the Natural History Museum in London. But while I could happily present a more exhaustive anthology of female phycologists from the 1800s to the present day, I have digressed enough from a guide to seaweed in the kitchen.

Ulva lactuca (Sea lettuce)

CHAPTER SIX

FARMING AND THE SEAWEED INDUSTRY

Over the centuries seaweed has been used as animal fodder and green manure for potatoes and other crops. One of the benefits of seaweed is that it is free from weeds and spores of crop disease. In winter storms, kelp is ripped off the seabed, carried ashore and thrown onto the beach in high piles. Farmers and crofters gather the seaweed for manure and dry the kelp stipes for valuable alginates, though far from the scale achieved at the height of the British kelp industry. Storm-cast seaweed reduces the impact of wind and waves, and protects beaches and dune fronts from erosion. Rotting seaweed is useful too. It abounds in sand flies and other invertebrates, and provides rich feeding for flocks of starlings, waders, gulls and other birds.

The name Canon Angus MacQueen was mentioned to me on many occasions while I was researching *Seaweed in the Kitchen*. Canon MacQueen, the youngest of seven children, was born on the Outer Hebridean Isle of South Uist in 1923. He left the Island to go a Catholic seminary on the mainland at the age of thirteen, but returned to the Hebrides as a priest on Eriskay and, latterly, on the Isle of Barra. He collects and eats seaweed. For centuries, crofters have collected seaweed from the shore and ploughed it into the Machair (the land by the sea which is rich in sand blown in by Atlantic winds). The seaweed used by the crofters as manure are the kelps, *Laminaria digitata* and *L. hyperborea*. The Islanders refer to it as 'tangle'. Canon MacQueen described tangle as a wonderful fertiliser from the ocean. He painted a magical picture of summers as a boy on the north end of South Uist, describing a barefooted childhood from March to October. The children delivered the cows to the Machair gate and were in charge of them until dusk. Having taken a note of the activities of the bull and cows to report back to their parents, the children enjoyed long summer days on the Machair and seashore. Canon MacQueen recalled that his mother would give him a home-baked scone with homemade cheese, butter or 'crowdie' to eat for lunch. His blue eyes twinkled as he recounted that, being youngsters, they would eat the 'piece' (lunch) on the road to the Machair:

> We never saw a human being until late at night, so as you can imagine these young barefooted people, with a shirt, no boots, stockings or underwear, who had eaten everything on the way to the Machair, were hungry by 11 o'clock. We had nothing to eat, we had eaten our pieces. We knew where to find water from spring wells, as people did hundreds of years before. We had plenty to drink, but we were hungry.

The children ate what they could on the Machair, following

the seasons as they sucked the nectar from wild Machair flowers. The beauty of the Machair is that it works in harmony with nature. Beyond the Machair is the Atlantic, and it was here that Canon MacQueen went to swim and to find more food in amongst the *fermmain* (Gaelic for seaweed). As he put it: 'After a year or two you became an expert on what to eat and what not to eat. What to eat was nice things, like the baby seaweed on the tangle (kelp) – the dulse. We grew throughout the summer months feeding ourselves on seaweed.'

Ronnie MacInnes from the Isle of Eriskay recalls that in the 1980s each Eriskay family had its own rock allocation from which they picked carragen. Islanders used carragen in puddings and as a throat soother.

Peat is not, as many believe, synonymous with every Western Isle. On the Isle of Tiree they remedied this by burning dried animal dung and seaweed. Dulse was often chewed or smoked by coastal folk as they worked on the land. As the Revd David Landsborough noted: 'The Highlanders and Irish were much in the habit, before tobacco became so rife, of washing dulse in fresh water, drying it in the sun, rolling it up, and then chewing it as they now do tobacco. How much better had it been for them had they stuck to the use of the less nauseous, less filthy, less hurtful dulse.' Laver was eaten by Scots, Irish and West Country folk, but the heart of the British industry was in Wales.

THE KELP INDUSTRY

The word kelp in Europe referred to the calcined ashes of seaweed or potash; this definition is still found in the Oxford dictionary. In the eighteenth century an alkali extract from kelp, soda, which was used in the manufacture of soap and glass, was a significant factor in the economy of the Northern and Western Isles. Competition came from Spanish barilla, which was prepared from the coastal plant, glasswort (*Salicornia spp*). Although comparable, the kelp soda (potash) was not as good in respect of yield or quality as barilla. During the American War of Independence and the Napoleonic Wars, the price of kelp was pushed up to £22 a ton. The production of potash from kelp was arduous. Over twenty tons of kelp, usually oarweed, had to be collected, dried and burned to produce just one ton of ash. The trustees of Scottish estates exploited the blockade on barilla as a lucrative opportunity to increase kelp production, and encouraged tenants to move to the coast or from the mainland to the Islands. Crofters and cottars licensed as kelp burners were employed to harvest the large quantity of seaweed that was washed up on the shore by storms, or to gather it at low tide. Whole families were involved in this backbreaking process, for which they earned £6 to £10 a season. This profited the landowners hugely, and to some extent the Islanders by providing employment. The author and naturalist Patrick Neill writing in 1806 said, 'the state of the agriculture is very low. The landowners pay attention to nothing but the manufacture of kelp. Kelp will be the ruin of Orkney'. Neill acknowledged that the comparative value of kelp was far greater than any income from crofting. There is even an argument that by gathering seaweed on the foreshore, crofters extended the legal boundaries of the landowners.

The value of kelp at the time is demonstrated by a dispute over ownership of the small Isle of Grianam, between the Outer Hebridean Isle of Harris and the Isle of Berneray, which could only be forded at low tide. The case was dragged through the Scottish Court Session from 1766 to 1771 simply because Grianam was surrounded by rich kelp beds. In hot weather, kelp could be burned within forty-eight hours, but in wet weather it had to be covered to stop the rain from washing out the soda.

The Battle of Waterloo signalled an end to the kelp boom. The cheaper barilla could once again be imported from Europe, and there was no longer a market for Hebridean kelp. Its price was lowered further by the discovery of large deposits of sulphate of potash in Germany and a cheap way of producing soda from salt. The poor kelpers suffered as the price of kelp went down to £2 a ton. With the failure of the kelp industry the landowners faced ruin. Estates changed hands and rack-renting forced many to abandon their homes. For the landlords, there were no overheads, and little need to pay the kelpers more than the minimum. By reserving rights of using the kelp when letting the land, landlords were able to set the kelpers to work on their own terms. Tenants were forced to work solely on the landlord's kelp by indirect economic pressure i.e. rents were fixed at such a level that they could be paid only by industrial work. As kelp began to bring in more than cattle, the balance of the traditional agricultural economy was disturbed.

The truck system (where workers were paid in kind) ensured that the landlords profited hugely. In *Scotland and the Scotch* (1849), Catherine Sinclair writes: 'Nothing can be more depressing than to witness the ruinous effects produced in Skye by the disuse of kelp.' The kelpers had earned an arduous if slightly better living from seaweed to the detriment of their crofts, from which they were then evicted. As the Scottish historian Tom Devine noted, Duncan Shaw was the first factor (land manager) to transport poverty-stricken families to North America in 1827, in what is now known as 'The Clearances'. In an article for *Longman's Magazine* entitled 'Among the Kelpers', Duncan J Robertson described the work poetically with skylark idyll: 'For spring and summer are the kelper's seasons, and long, dry days, which scorch and wither the young crops, are welcome to the crofter who has secured a good stock of "tangles" in winter.' However, even Robertson mentions kelp and inclement weather. The two often went hand in hand.

In 1812, the French chemist Bernard Courtois added sulphuric acid to kelp ash, and first note is made of the purple vapour, iodine. The *Laminaria* species accumulate iodine in their tissues and its use in medicine revived the kelp industry. During this phase of the European seaweed industry, a brilliant chemist, Edward Charles Cortis Stanford gave the kelp industry a new lease of life on the Isle of Tiree. Stanford's prize-winning lecture, entitled *On the Economic Applications of Seaweed* (1862) was a chemical and botanical review of seaweed, but also extolled its industrial virtues. He was passionate, but his obsession with seaweed was profitable. Stanford leased the kelp shores on the Isle of Tiree and Coll from the Duke of Argyll and invested in Glassary, a factory on Tiree and another in Clydebank, Glasgow. He encountered the ubiquitous problem of Inner Hebridean infrastructure (not without its counterpart today), and communication was difficult, because the Islanders spoke Gaelic – but Stanford persevered.

The production of iodine flourished once Stanford had convinced the people of Tiree that it would be preferable to burn kelp in closed retorts (glassware) without air, rather than in open pits i.e. by destructive distillation. Stanford later discovered algin, a carbohydrate similar to cellulose, and all of this because he was a seaweed enthusiast. However, the production of good quality potash from kelp was laborious, and so when sources of iodine, soda and potash were discovered in Strassfurt in Germany, and in the deserts of northern Chile, the British kelp industry could no longer compete and went into its second decline.

The third phase of the industry was again in part due to the pioneer seaweed researcher Edward Charles Cortis Stanford – this time through his identification of algin, or alginic acid, though it was not until 1923 that extracts of brown seaweeds containing alginate were produced commercially and sold as thickening and gelling agents. The British Algin Company Ltd (1885), Blandola Ltd (1908), and Liverpool Borax Ltd (1909) were involved in a fairly crude alginate, as was Thornley Binder Ltd. With Thornley's move to San Diego in 1927 came the Kelp Products Corporation, and eventually Kelco Company, which produced alginate as a commercial product. During the Second World War, the Cefoil seaweed factory in West Kintyre exploited sodium alginate for the war effort: it was used to make camouflage paint and parachute silk. There is also reference to algin paper, which could be safely eaten and which was developed for secret documents.

In Britain, the kelp industry is synonymous with Scotland, but the gathering of kelp was important in Ireland too. The seaweed species dulse/dillisk and carrageen have always been acceptable as food in Ireland, and seaweed was also used in the Irish linen industry to bleach cloth. In common with Scotland, seaweed was involved in Irish glassmaking and the production of iodine.

Another Celtic country, Wales, also has a strong industrial association with seaweed. Early Roman descriptions of Britain tell of a wild island people who lived on simple foods: milk, shellfish, wild plants and occasional meat. Traditionally the working class ate these simple and filling foods. Welsh workers did indeed obtain protein from dairy products, but where available, particularly in South Wales, this included cockles and laverbread. The Burry Estuary, located between the Gower peninsula and Llanelli in South Wales, includes large intertidal areas where cockles and laver are still important industries today. At low tide, the tidal movement uncovers large areas of rock and sand, exposing laver and cockling beds. In Penclawdd and around Carmarthen Bay, commercial harvesting of shellfish and laver has given rise to a thriving processing industry.

Although laver is also collected and eaten in Ireland, Scotland, Devon, Cornwall, the Isle of Man and the Channel Islands (where it may be called by a different name), Wales is Britain's commercial point of reference. Laverbread is an age-old Welsh art, which many feel needs to be protected before it becomes muddled into the latest food fashion. Today, laverbread may be ordered from suppliers such as Selwyn's Seaweed of Penclawdd, where the packaging is bilingual, in Welsh and English. This is a nationalist statement but laverbread is very much a South Wales delicacy.

Those who live on the edge of the sea look to it for nourishment – in Wales, it is laver that provides this. It was traditionally a peasant food, but it is one that reached the gentlemen's clubs of nineteenth century London. As a niche heritage product it is once again creating new waves, with business potential for artisanal food producers. The recent British appreciation of Japanese sushi may have helped in the resurgence of interest in laver.

Nori, which is used in sushi, was once known as gamblers' grass, because its harvest was very much a hit-or-miss affair. An Englishwoman, Dr Kathleen Drew (after her marriage she was known as Kathleen Drew Baker), provided the answer to the mysterious life cycle of nori and, significantly, she made the discovery while studying laver on Welsh beaches. Prior to Drew's research a successful nori harvest could not be guaranteed. Wales may have played a part in the research of nori, but laverbread is made from British laver, which is not the same as nori. Professor Juliet Brodie of the Natural History Museum attests that amanori or nori harvested from the seaweeds cultivated in Japan cannot be equated to British laver. This is simply because they are not from the same group of seaweeds. Laver is a species of the genus *Porphyra* and nori comes from a species of the genus *Pyropia*, typically *Pyropia yezoensis* or *Pyropia tenera*. Professor Brodie, an international authority on *Porphyra,* commented that this species is probably extinct in the wild. Nori is farmed in Japan – so wild British laver is not nori. It would be on a par to calling English sparkling wine champagne.

The production of Welsh laverbread is a skilled process that has been handed down for generations. In the 1800s, laver collection was arduous, but it was nevertheless an important cottage industry and a source of local employment in South Wales. Historically, families collected laver by hand from October to May, and loaded the full panniers onto donkeys. The laver was then soaked and washed free of sand. Before hosepipes, it was washed in streams, draped over the roof of the family laver hut, and left to dry. The dried laver was then taken by horse and cart to Swansea to be processed. With the improvements to nineteenth century infrastructure it was sent by rail. Laver is now sourced on the north and south Welsh coastlines, but much of the production is still on the Gower peninsula. Traditionally, the laver was washed by hand and cooked in pans over open fires. Although production is now industrialised, traditional methods are still honoured and it remains an important cottage industry.

Today, harvesters pick laver by hand throughout the year and rinse it in seawater. It is then transported to a processor. Selwyn's Seaweed, a family-run company founded in 1950, still uses local seaweed pickers. It processes and cans the laver, or sells it in clear wrapped trays. The company also sells frozen laverbread – laver freezes superbly. Another company, Parsons Pickles processes laverbread in partnership with Penclawdd Shellfish Processing. Both laverbread companies sell shellfish too. Cockles and laver grow and cook well together. Ingredients that grow in close proximity pair well on a plate.

In order to authenticate the origin of the seaweed, a movement document records the name and address of the gatherer, where the laver was gathered, the quantity and date of gathering, and the date of its delivery to the processor – and there is a dated signature on delivery by both collector and processor. The traceability of the laver for Welsh laverbread is assured. After collection, the laver is washed repeatedly in water to remove sand and foreign bodies. This is either done by hand or by machine. The laver is then drained well. Large fronds of laver are roughly chopped, and then the laver is cooked as soon as possible. When cooked, the seaweed – depending upon its moisture content – is either drained or placed directly into a mincing machine and puréed. If a more textured laverbread is required, the laver is roughly chopped. After cooking and mincing, the seaweed is put in shallow trays and into a chiller. Finished product units are either canned or packed into sterile containers, which are chilled prior to dispatch. Tinned laverbread is available from delicatessens, food halls, or online. Fresh laverbread is on sale in Welsh supermarkets, local markets and in fishmongers. On a smaller scale, laver is also available from market stalls or fishmonger counters in Devon and Cornwall, where it is collected locally.

In Wales, laver features on both local and fine dining menus, but it is traditional as a savoury cake on the Welsh breakfast plate. The laverbread eaten at breakfast is composed of cooked laver, which has been rolled in oatmeal and fried in bacon fat until crisp. Increasingly, chefs are using laver in exciting recipes, well beyond breakfast and the traditional lamb sauce. This bodes well for the shellfish and laver industry, which absorbed some of the unemployment resulting from the closure of the South Wales mining pits. A street food business has also raised the profile of laver. Café Mor, which sells imaginative and delicious seafood (including laver), was set up in 2010, and was voted overall winner in the 2011 British Street Food Awards. Under a new company name, The Pembrokeshire Beach Food Company, it won the Best Street Food/Takeaway category in the 2014 Radio 4 Food and Farming Awards. The new company combines local seafood with foraged ingredients, and sells Welshman's Caviar (dried flakes of laver), amongst other seashore products, from its online shop.

Seaweed aquaculture at its most basic is a means of providing employment opportunities in developing countries with suitable coastal environments. A contemporary aquaculture has grown up in Africa and India, as well as the East Asia and the Pacific. Farming seaweed requires low technology input and uses a natural resource for financial benefit. China is the world's largest producer of aquaculture species (including seaweeds). Sadly, nature does not only give, it also takes away. The 2013 super typhoon Yolanda hit the Philippines and left a trail of destruction in the multimillion-dollar seaweed industry in the northernmost part of Bohol. Relying on a natural resource means that high demand can't always be met. The 2011 Fukushima nuclear power plant disaster impacted on seaweed supplies in Japan. A direct result of polluted seaweed beds was that Japan increased trade with other seaweed producing countries. Maine in the USA and Ireland amongst other countries benefited. It was, however, always thus. Germany was a competitive source of potash (kelp) in the nineteenth century, and continues its seaweed industry tradition as the largest EU importer and processor of seaweed from developing countries. Those interested in the seaweed industry might also visit Brittany, where seaweed gathering dates back to Neolithic times. The eco-museum at Plouguerneau is historically insightful, and there is an annual *Fête du Goemon* ('Seaweed festival') near Esquibien in Western Brittany. Bretons dress in traditional costume to re-enact the old method of gathering and burning seaweed in open kilns.

The historical use of seaweed as fertiliser and in industry has been noted, but modern-day seaweed is seen as a potential solution to the world's fuel and food problems. Seaweed is at the bottom of the food chain and has no food supply conflict. It has no need for real land estate, water or pesticides, and has an ability to grow faster than terrestrial plants. Aquaculture may increase food production by what is known as 'the blue revolution'. This is the water equivalent of the green revolution, the management of water resources to enable food and fuel security. Proponents highlight the fact that seaweed cleans the water in which it grows i.e. it has the ability to bio-accumulate nutrients and pollutants including heavy metals. Because seaweed grows quickly, scientists anticipate that its oils and starches, when cheaply processed into biodiesel or ethanol, will in time rival fossil fuels. Mark Edwards, an Arizona State University agribusiness professor, is one such enthusiast. His book *Green Algae Strategy: End Oil Imports and Engineer Sustainable Food and Fuel* is available free of charge on the internet. At Edwards' 60th birthday dinner party, his wife Ann prepared a seven-course meal in which each course included seaweed. Edwards lives his seaweed dream and has a number of interesting seaweed websites with a selection of recipes. He recommended that I try a smoothie and a tofu recipe which included fresh water algae, namely chlorella and spirulina.

Macroalgae are commonly known as seaweeds, and microalgae such as spirulina are often called 'phytoplankton'. As the word implies they are not normally visible without a microscope. The Hebridean Seaweed Company on Lewis, and Asco on North Uist, are two companies that commercially harvest knotted wrack (*Ascophyllum nodosum*). In their 2012 'Seaweed Survey of the Outer Hebrides', undertaken for the Crown Estate, Juliet Brodie and Jo Wilbraham noted positively that the impact of this harvesting on diversity was low. It seems, however, to be widely accepted that the removal of seaweed has the potential to alter the dynamics of the ecosystem. The predominant seaweed harvested is knotted wrack, which is in abundant supply on the Hebrides. Asco (an abbreviation of *Ascophyllum nodosum*) is a relatively new company that sells seaweed that is dried over organic woodchips to, amongst other places, Dubai, where it is fed to camels. Smaller companies such as Argyll-based Seaweed Organics hand harvest seaweed for their beauty products. Mara Seaweed is an artisan company with sustainable ethics that is making headway in the higher end of the retail market. Just Seaweed on the Isle of Bute is one of the few businesses to offer both fresh and dried seaweed. The Cornish Seaweed Company, Seaspoon, New Wave Foods and Atlantic Kitchen also sell dried seaweed. Kate Burns runs a company called Islander Kelp with her son. It is based on Rathlin Island off the north coast or Ireland and is growing the UK's first kelp on ropes. Rathlin has a population of around a hundred, and Burns hopes that her business will serve as a diversification for the fishing industry. Her family is fourth generation fisher folk. Having first relied on natural spores in the water to spawn the kelp that grows on the ropes, the company has now set up a laboratory to germinate their own miniature kelp, which are then transferred onto the ropes.

Integrated multi-trophic aquaculture (IMTA) is a practice whereby the by-products (wastes) from one species are recycled to become inputs (fertilizers, food and energy) for another. The Scottish Association for Marine Science (SAMS) is researching this concept with farmed salmon waste. The waste is assimilated by seaweed, which is also of commercial value. It appears to amount to eco-friendly recycling, which seems to be a win-win scenario. Pilot research by SAMS suggests seaweeds with a high potential for development in IMTA include kelps, dulse and *Ulva spp.* This work is in its early research stages, but brings sustainability to the forefront of the Scottish seaweed industry.

A project to cultivate the seaweeds dulse, laver and oarweed for human consumption is well underway in Ireland. Results are promising and dulse has been grown for the first time on vertically deployed nets, where the dulse appears as a curtain of seaweed in the seawater. Dulse is of significant value because it enables pickers of the wild product to augment supplies with farmed. A regular supply of dulse is not guaranteed and this is not aided by the fact that it remains malleable when dried. Sites for seaweed farming require careful consideration and are dependent on the needs of the seaweed species (such as current, water depth, salinity and nutrients). Farms must also respect other coastal users and the regulations governing Special Areas of Conservation.

The risk of invasive seaweeds muscling in on the seabed, or natural disasters such as typhoon devastation, is outside the seaweed industry's control, but man must be attentive to warming seas, climate change and unforeseen circumstances. In 2014 the total production of nori in Saga, Kumamoto and Fukuoka prefectures in the Ariake Sea dropped about 20 %, or about 800 million sheets. The seaweed harvest began well in the autumn of 2013, but 'red tide', caused by plankton, emerged in January and spread in February. Red tide saps all nutrients, such as nitrogen and phosphorus, and this causes a loss of colour. One assessment of why the red tide had occurred was as follows: 'We had dry weather with little rain in January, which may have promoted photosynthesis. But the real cause is not known.' This sentence is poignant; we still have much to learn about seaweed and aquaculture. Harvesting wild seaweed is becoming an increasingly profitable business proposition, and weather and tides aside there is little outlay or inherent risk, but wild seaweed is a valuable resource and it is time for cautious regulation. In April 2014 the Marine Stewardship Council (MSC) announced that it is expanding its sustainability standard to include seaweed. This will hopefully provide a benchmark for those gathering seaweed to work towards. Indigenous seaweed is fast growing and does not harm the environment or other native species, but in our quest for a sustainable future we need to become seaweed savvy before we pillage something that is still considered by many to be a weed.

Each week seems to bring a new seaweed product to the market place. In 2014, a cheesemaker based in Ceredigion, Wales, added seaweed to a botanical gin, and is marketing the product as being 'unique in colour and flavour', due to seaweed's seasonal variation. Isle of Harris Gin has sugar kelp as its key ingredient, and Isle of Barra Atlantic Gin focuses on carrageen. Another novel idea to hit the British market is nori cupcake wrappers. Kelpie is the name of a Scottish Ale that contains not kelp, as the name might suggest, but bladder wrack. The name is apt, as in Scottish folklore a kelpie is a mystical shape-shifting water spirit. The ale itself has its origins in coastal alehouses. Another bottle with a similar name is Celp, which contains seaweed-infused Islay whisky. Tångkorn is a caviar-style product made from seaweed, on sale in IKEA. I asked which seaweed was used in Tångkorn, but drew a blank. I'm sure that consumers will, as seaweed increases in popularity, ask this same question. Studies have shown that the addition of seaweed in foods has a preservative effect, and so reduces the need to add salt (Gupta et al, 2010). Acting on this premise, Seagreens used *Ascophyllum nodosum* as a salt replacement in wholemeal bread during trials at Sheffield Hallam University. It was found that the bread's shelf life was extended by up to nine days when compared with bread baked without seaweed. There was, however, no significant suppression of mould when seaweed was added to white bread dough. The Hallam research follows the work of the German scientist, Dr Heinrich Lienau, who experimented with seaweed in Iceland in the 1930s. Lienau noted that bread made from seaweed flour was not only non-fattening, but it also retained its freshness. The Second World War interrupted Lienau's seaweed-bread research, and when he returned to Germany in 1939 he was sent to a concentration camp in Sachsenhausen. He survived the ordeal and, encouraged by fellow Norwegian prisoners, became the first man in Europe to bake bread from the sea using dried Norwegian seaweed. Adding seaweed may increase the nutritional value of a food product, but both the Sheffield Hallam study and Lienau's research suggests that seaweed adds shelf life value.

Fermentation is increasingly popular with home cooks who make sourdough bread and those who enjoy a good blue cheese. Fermented food is an ancient cooking process with a history stretching back thousands of years. However, few studies have been conducted in relation to obtaining fermentation-related food products from seaweed. A paper by Motoharu Uchida introduced three topics on seaweed fermentation: one for alcohol beverages or possibly biofuel, a second for marine silage using blooming algae *Ulva spp*, and the third, a fermented seaweed sauce. Fermented sauce products are usually produced from soy and fish, but in this study the seaweed nori (*Pyropia yezoensis*) was used. There is a fermented recipe using dulse on page 221 – it works.

Unpasteurized foods are said to aid digestion and boost immunity. Beyond experiments within the home encouraged by the author Sandor Katz, current research is looking at using seaweed as a substrate for lactic acid and ethanol fermentation. This could lead to the development of food from seaweed fermentation in vogue with fermented foods made from terrestrial ingredients such as rice, soybean, vegetables and milk. Seaweed sauce is one possible product for development. The setting and stabilising properties of seaweed are well documented, but new uses for marine algae are evolving daily. Sadly, the work of Lienau demonstrates that – until recently – seaweed research takes many years to become mainstream. The commonplace acceptance of a fifth taste, umami is a case in point. But to conclude on a positive note: my Hebridean seaweed sourdough starter has been received with enthusiasm and is thriving in kitchens over 500 miles away.

The very thought of E numbers often makes people who cook from scratch look anxious. To simply say that seaweed is only used in ice cream and to give head to beer, barely scratches the surface of its complex chemical use by the food industry. Alginates are the principal structural polysaccharide components of brown seaweeds (just as cellulose is the principal carbohydrate in land plants). The commercial product is extracted from a wide range of brown seaweed species: notably kelps and knotted wrack. The alginate in seaweed is a mixed salt of sodium, potassium, calcium and magnesium, and its extraction involves ion exchange in an alkaline medium, followed by precipitation, purification and recovery of the alginic acid. The exact composition is dependent on the state of the raw seaweed. Alginates are used in the food industry as a stabiliser for beer, ice cream, yogurt, cream, and cheese, and as a thickener and emulsifier for salad, puddings, jam, tomato juice, and canned products.

E406 or Agar agar is obtained from major genera of red seaweeds, including *Gelidium* and *Gracilaria* often from Argentina, Canada, Chile, China, France, India, Indonesia, Japan, Madagascar, Mexico, Morroco, Namibia, New Zealand, Peru, Portugal, South Africa, Spain, Thailand and the USA. The agar is extracted using hot, dilute alkali and then cooled to form a very firm brittle gel, which is frozen to disrupt the gel structure. When the gel is thawed, impurities dissolved in the water are expelled using high pressure and then the gel is dried and ground to produce powdered agar. The strength of gel given by agar is variable, depending on its origin. This makes it necessary to test batches of agar for gel strength before use, and supports my thought that some wild carrageen has better gelling potential than others. Slender wart weed (*Gracilaria gracilis*) may grow in some British waters, but its identification requires expertise. Agar agar was first produced in the sixteenth century in the remote mountainous areas of Japan, where it is called *kanten,* which translates as 'frozen skies' because the gel froze naturally. In a 1987 academic article on the production, properties and uses of agar, Rafael Armisén and Fernando Galatas documented an account of a Japanese officer visiting a small inn in the Japanese mountains, where he ate a traditional seaweed jelly dish, prepared by cooking *Gelidium* with water. After dinner, the innkeeper threw the surplus jelly outside. The jelly froze during the night, then thawed and dried in the sun, leaving a dry white residue. When this was boiled in water and cooled it produced a clearer jelly than was originally produced. *Kanten* describes the natural method of freeze-thawing. Microbiological laboratories use agar as a culture medium and require large quantities of agar. It is also used in processed foodstuffs.

Carrageenans (E407) are extracted from red seaweeds (*Rhodophyceae*). In Britain, *Chondrus crispus* and *Mastocarpus stellatus* grow on much of the shoreline and are a good source of gelling carrageen. They contain a mix of carrageenan types, the predominant ones being kappa and lambda. *Gigartina spp* and *Irdaea* are also harvested in the wild. *Eucheuma* is a Pacific species and the largest commercial source of it is harvested in the Philippines where it is farmed. Processed *Eucheuma* also has an E number: E407A. During production, the E407 extract is filtered to remove cellulose from the seaweed, but these are present in E407A so it gives cloudy gels in water. Alan Imeson, a food scientist tells me that E407A is used in processed hams, pork and poultry in Russia and Central and Eastern Europe, to gel water in meat. Its use is not, however, widespread in Western Europe. Here, foods declare the stabiliser or gelling agent i.e. carrageenan rather than an E number.

Most of the seaweed from which carrageenan is extracted

is farmed rather than wild. Carrageenans are used as gelling agents, thickening agents and stabilisers. In dairy products, they are used to form gels with a range of textures, to thicken milk drinks and to stabilise neutral ph dairy products. Carrageenan is also used to form water jellies, frequently in combination with locust bean gum. Different species of seaweed give different carrageenan types on extraction. These are labelled as kappa, iota and lambda, each of which has a different chemical structure, which results in differences in gel texture (setting). Kappa types are the strongest and most brittle; iota produce soft gels; and lambda types are non-gelling, used to thicken liquids and modify food texture.

Commercial products often blend more than one carrageenan type to produce the required texture. Dr Alan Imeson tells me that no declaration is made in the USA, so foods with carrageenan may contain any combination. Professor Mike Guiry suggests that the choice of agars, carrageenans or alginates used as a binder or emulsifier is either down to food technologists' preferences or for specific rheological properties ('rheology' originates from the Greek word 'rhei' meaning 'to flow' – it is the study of the flow behaviour of matter). Choice can be just a matter of national preference or proximity to a particular resource (i.e. down to historical factors). When wars interrupt supply, preferences change, as was the case of barilla and kelp during the Napoleonic Wars. More recently agar agar was in short supply due to blockades during the Second World War and some food processors in Europe and North America changed to use carrageenan. From the industrial, we now move to medicine and nutrition.

Sea-tangle tents with Laminaria digitata used for dilating the cervix

CHAPTER SEVEN

MEDICINE AND NUTRITION
(BY DR STEPHEN GLOVER BIRD)

It is no surprise to find that seaweeds have long been used for medicinal purposes. Both the physical property and mineral content give them an appeal for use as simple treatments. Seaweeds can hold water – acting to heat or cool tissue. They are resilient so they don't tend to disintegrate and sea water is a natural cleanser for wounds.

Macroalgae may look like sea vegetables but their structure and lifecycle make for very different properties than those of land-based plants. It is these novel properties that are renewing interest from both medical and industrial researchers into future developments and use. However, the high mineral content always did lend itself to the production of tinctures, potions, lotions and infusions, while the gelling properties and thin fibrous nature of the fronds made for easy use as rubs and compresses. All these were long the mainstay of both reputable physicians and local folklore. Coastal and island communities have had to make use of these properties as substitutes for the more commercial but less available advances in treatments, even until relatively recently.

Goitres or 'thicknecks' were managed in Highland Scotland with 'mantles' of seaweed, apparently applied to the neck with good effect. Presumably there was some absorption of iodine in the process. The serrated wracks were considered cure-alls, particularly for 'rheumatics', and were used in various ways, including localised applications in the form of hot-knotted bandages – not dissimilar in effect to the hot wax baths of today. Mediaeval medicine inherited such terms as 'falling of the uvula' from the ancient Greeks. It may have been associated with breathing difficulties, but certainly had bad connotations and was treated with particular rituals, including amulets of red seaweed tied around the neck while reciting a blessing.

Although not particularly palatable or digestible when raw, boiled seaweeds will have always had the same properties that they have today: soothing to the digestive system, plentiful in easily absorbed minerals, and, in gelatinous form, suitable for the toothless and aged, as well as the toothless and newly-born. It is interesting to note that seaweeds have been serious contenders as the basis for a number of favoured remedies, even in more modern times. Laminaria (kelp) 'sticks' are still used to 'ripen' the cervix of pregnant women to aid their labour (and even induce abortion). This is a refinement of the laminaria 'tents' first described by Sir James Simpson in 1865, nearly twenty years after he pioneered the use of chloroform. The folklore and fuzzy logic of past seaweed use still remains, but while the more recent claims for the properties of these macroalgae are intriguing, their future use will depend on the rigour of scientific proof. That being the case, recent studies do suggest benefits to treatments of viral infections, some cancer types and bone metabolism, for example. Antiviral properties have been found in extracts of *Dumontiaceae,* as well as other red seaweeds. It is thought that this is due to the properties of galactans (long-chain sugars), which are chemicals particular to red algal species. There are indeed seaweed extracts available on the market for use against viral cold sores (herpes simplex). These natural products do seem to shorten individual flare-ups, but do not stop recurrence or spread, so they have no great advantage over conventional treatments. Likewise, the fucoidans found largely in brown seaweeds may have some antiviral but, more pertinently, some anticancer properties.

The Chinese have used seaweeds to reduce swellings, including presumed cancers, for hundreds of years, but it is only recently that formal studies are indicating how fucoidans might act as promoters or inhibitors of the various chemical activities within cells. These fucoidans seem to have the advantage of being natural products that are easily taken up, but with the potential for either having a direct action themselves, or – by indirectly helping other active molecules – on their target within cells. There is certainly evidence that fucoidans affect what is known as 'apoptosis'. Apoptosis is the natural life and death cycle of cell tissues. This is a key element of cancers and their control. It is also possible that seaweed polysaccharides (the more general term for long-chain sugars) help to block hormones that play an important part in particular cancers, such as breast and prostate, but again the mechanism for this has not yet been demonstrated. The prospects are good, but (at the time of writing) the proof is still lacking.

As well as their chemical properties, the physical potential for alginates (from brown seaweeds) to bind into stable matrix formations, utilised in the new technology of three-dimensional printing, is proving an opportunity for limb joint-surface reconstruction, bone remineralisation and even heart valve replacements. In fact, creating shapes from durable tissues that are inexpensive and safe has the potential to alter dramatically all sorts of medical treatments.

In complementary medicine, seaweeds play a notable part, with many recipes for tonics and appetite stimulants, while at the other end of the scale, fucoxanthin, a Vitamin-A-like orange pigment found in many brown seaweeds, is marketed as a slimming agent. Seaweed extract is prepared in many forms, from tonics and supplements to aperients and hair-restorants, all to aid wellbeing and promote recovery from illness.

The surgical potential for seaweed extracts already includes absorbent wound dressings, which have been commercially available since the 1980s. They boast the 'Goldilocks quality' of keeping wounds not too moist while not too dry.

Nutrition is sometimes seen to be on the soft end of scientific research but our dietary habits have, as we know, a profound effect on the landscape and, in this case, potentially the shore-scape. We must get our investment into seaweed use right. Seaweeds do have the potential to aid health and contribute to a varied and well-balanced diet. Targeted funding is merited for further academic research while chefs and home-cooks should certainly add it to – and keep it on – their ingredients list.

NUTRITION

Seaweed in its natural state definitely contains a variety of well-known and beneficial nutrients. The argument for seaweed in our diet can certainly be made on the grounds of taste – hence this book. However, the more prosaic demands of global health and human nutrition require a more dispassionate assessment of all the qualities of seaweed.

It is all too easy to make assumptions about many foodstuffs, whether concerning their production or their consumption, and indeed the economics and the ethics of the food industry are rarely straightforward, and this is also true of seaweeds. To illustrate this there is a wealth of literature detailing the nutritional value of edible seaweeds, but which is mostly based on analysis of the 'proximate composition' of key groups. (This is analysis by crude breakdown of foodstuffs into five basic components: Moisture, Ash, Protein, Fat and Carbohydrate – this analysis is not even derived from direct measurement: the Carbohydrate composition is calculated by extrapolation from the others.)

It should be noted that nutrient composition is highly variable, both within and between species, as well as across localities and through the seasons (see Table 1, right).

Edible seaweeds, when considered as 'wholefoods', do indeed provide a rich and balanced source of key macro- and micro-nutrients such as fibre, other (long-chain) carbohydrates, proteins with their amino acids, antioxidants, polyunsaturated fatty acids, vitamins and minerals.

These nutrients can be found at levels similar to, or often greater than, other wholefood sources. However, information regarding the bioavailability of seaweed-derived nutrients in humans is limited. A few studies have looked at the available levels of key trace elements and heavy metals from wild harvested European seaweeds using 'in vitro' (laboratory-based rather than living tissue-based) testing. A few commercially available prepared food products have also been investigated. In general, these studies show the bioavailability of minerals and trace elements from differing seaweed species to be highly variable.

As an illustration of the complexity surrounding risks and benefits of seaweeds in our diet there has been a real concern about arsenic, which gets absorbed and concentrated in seaweeds growing on some shorelines. In fact, arsenic, one of the heavy metals, appears in both mineral (inorganic) forms as well as organic (bound into living tissue compound) forms.

		total carbohydrate	total fibre *	total protein	total minerals	key minerals	key vitamins	amino acid score ***
		% composition of dried seaweed						
Common names	Scientific name							
kelp oarweed	Laminaria digitata	38-61	30-38	3-20	15-45	Ca, Mg, K, Na	A, C, E	31
sugar kelp kombu royale	Saccharina latissima	38-61	27-31	3-20	15-45	Ca, Mg, K, Na, I	B1	31
Atlantic wakame winged kelp	Alaria esculenta	46-51	40	9-21		Ca, Mg, Na	A, C, K	
sea spaghetti sea harricots	Himanthalia elongata	32-61	20-48	5-24	20-30	Ca, Mg, Na	A, C, E	
wracks	Fucus vesciculosus F. serratus F. spiralis	45-71	10-54	3-20	7-30	Ca, K, S, Mg, Na	E	
Jap weed ** wire weed	Sargassum muticum	4-68	49-62	9-20	14-44			82
Laver nori sleabach sloke	Porphyra spp.	40-76	24-49	7-50	7-35	P, Mn, Fe, Cu, Zn	A, B1, B2, C, E	91
dulse	Palmaria palmata	38-74	20-34	8-36	12-37	P, K, Mn, Fe, Cu, Zn, Se	A, B1, B2, beta carotene, C, E	
pepper dulse	Osmundia pinnatifida							
sea lettuce gut weed	Ulva spp	15-65	22-54	1.5-41	11-55	Ca, Mg, Mn, Fe, Zn	A, B2, Beta carotene, C, E	
velvet horn	Codium fragile							

Table 1. Nutritional composition of European seaweeds, Sarah Hotchkiss (2013). The information contained in this table is based on data for European seaweeds harvested from different locations and at different times of the year and thus a range of values is presented.

While the inorganic arsenic remains very toxic (as an effective poison), it is found in low (and usually safe) quantities in raw seaweeds; the organic forms of arsenic, which do occur in higher concentrations, have little if any toxic effect on mammals, including humans. While neither form is desirable in our diet, this is reassuring. Consumption of seaweed is generally very safe. From a wider perspective there is a possibility that seawaters polluted with other heavy metals could be effectively cleansed by regular harvesting and safe disposal of exposed seaweed beds.

It is not just the detailed nutritional content of seaweed species that needs our attention, but how their use can affect the whole of our diet. Other stabilising properties of certain species could have intriguing benefits.

If you want to pursue some scientific findings in your own kitchen you could try out the useful property of sea spaghetti (*Himanthalia digitata*), now available in supermarkets, as an enhancer of shelf or fridge life for home cooking and baking.[1] The active ingredient is best extracted from the raw seaweed using alcohol. I am not sure how easy it is to produce this refinement in the kitchen, but it might be fun trying. Commercial food producers are starting to extend freshness using just such techniques. You can try a straightforward option – see Fiona's bread recipe, for example on page 217.

Indeed the effect of foods (and medicines) on gut bacteria is emerging as a key area for research. Recent studies have shown that these bugs themselves are quite responsive to the foods we eat, and this itself influences our risks for Non-Communicable Diseases (NCDs) like Diabetes and Cardiovascular Disease (heart attacks and strokes) – still the main cause of death in developed countries. It is the unrefined foods, such as fruit and vegetables as well as the edible seaweeds, that seem to provide protection, most probably by enhancing a good balance of gut flora.

There is compelling evidence that we should include seaweeds

---

1. 'An assessment of the antioxidant and antimicrobial activity of six species of edible Irish seaweeds', *International Food Research Journal* **17**: **205-220** (*2010*).

in all forms, raw, cooked, dried and refined in the western diet.[2]

However, the complex proteins and carbohydrates integral to the fibrous structure of seaweeds seem to restrict the availability of some of these key nutrients. Further study is required, not least into how humans absorb the nutrients in seaweed, and of course into the commercial and environmental viability of large-scale harvesting.

Dried seaweeds should be made more of in condiment form, as part of a reduced salt diet. For me, dulse has a salty bacon-like flavour, but the (ever) green alva and sea lettuce provide stronger colour and flavour alternatives – to salt in particular. We can, and should, all get used to less saltiness in our food and a sprinkle of these is simply more flavoursome. But unless you dry it for yourself this is not a cheap option.

If the coastal regions (of the UK) could start to familiarise locals to the use of fresh seaweed then we could address the challenges of providing sustainable, inexpensive, nutritious and, yes, really tasty alternatives to existing food options. The mineral content is substantial and varied. The only cautions being that sustained high intake of iodine (over months) is not kind to thyroid glands, and large single intake of potassium can, in rare cases, affect cardiac stability.[3]

The very distinct characteristics of seaweeds have made for extravagant claims for the benefits they can bring, whether as food, medicine or as industrial raw material. These are indeed exciting times for those interested in seaweeds (phycologists), but none of us should take extravagant and unsupported claims without, so to speak, a pinch of salt.

There are new and updated publications being produced regularly which give more detailed information at a more scientific level for those interested.[4]

2. *'Dietary seaweed and human health'*. Culinary Arts and Sciences VII: Global, National and Local Perspectives, **8 May 2012.**
3. *'Palmaria palmata (Dulse) as an unusual maritime aetiology of hyperkalemia in a patient with chronic renal failure: a case report',* Journal of Medical Case Reports, **2010.**
4. Seaweed in Health and Disease Prevention, **Joel Fleurence & Ira Levine, Academic Press, 2016.**

Royal fern seaweed on a salad spinner, with Errant Bunny Ears
(Lomentaria aerticulata) **and Pepper dulse** *(Osmundea pinnatifida)*

RECIPES

I've included one or two recipes here which are best described as 'Recipe writing with scissors', i.e. they are taken from scrapbooks. Such recipes were clipped out and saved – and often stained from frequent use. Seaweed was an acceptable ingredient in the culture of the Irish and Scots, and both carrageen and dulse feature in the recipes of immigrant Celtic Americans and Canadians. Sadly, such recipes are few. Seaweed deserves better. Let's campaign for its return to our tables, and endorse the sentiments of Lord Boyd Orr, director of the Rowett Nutrition Institute in Aberdeen in the early 1920s, who wrote: 'Up until the middle of the last [nineteenth] century, the people of Scotland were eating natural foodstuffs. With the introduction of machinery, this has been changed...Natural foods have been changed into artificial foodstuffs, with the very best substances purified away that the Almighty put there to keep us in perfect health.'

Seaweed is natural and some species taste very good. Hopefully, research will soon tell us that its nutrients are assured too.

A Gaelic proverb tells us *Lean gu dlùth ri cliù do shinnsre* ('Follow close the fame of your fathers'). In so doing, foragers should be mindful of the rules of the countryside, and wary of Dante's fourth circle of Hell – Greed. Pick enough for yourself, no more, and don't tug up any roots or holdfasts. That way, foraging for wild food can continue to be enjoyed by everyone.

Let's eat seaweed and heed the words of Mrs Gatty in her introduction to *British Sea-Weeds*: 'It sounds like a joke to say that a sea-weed collector should always order his dinner at high-tide hour, but the idea is a very good one, and, were there none but sea-weed collectors in a company, might be (under limits) carried out every day.'

FIRST COURSES

AVOCADO, EDAMAME BEAN AND DULSE BRUSCHETTA

Ingredients: (makes 15-20 depending on size):
1 ½ French style batons of bread
Extra Virgin Olive Oil
2 ripe avocados
2 tsps dried, finely ground dulse
Juice of half a small lemon
50 g cooked edamame beans
Freshly ground pepper
Additional dulse

Cut the bread on the diagonal into small slices. Lightly toast on each side. Brush one side with olive oil, sparingly. Pop the avocados in a bowl and mash with a fork. Add the dried dulse lemon juice, edamame beans and pepper to taste. Stir gently to combine. Spoon the mixture high onto each bruschetta slice. Drizzle olive oil over the avocado and edamame beans and sprinkle with dulse or beetroot and sugar kelp dust (see recipe on page 220). Serve as soon as possible.

CAWL LAWR

The author John Lewis-Stempel contributed this recipe. Vegetarians can replace the lamb stock with seaweed or vegetable stock.

Ingredients (serves 4):

75 g laver purée

75 g butter

1 large onion, peeled and chopped

3 medium potatoes, peeled and chopped

1 medium carrot, chopped

1.2 litres lamb stock

1 tsp white sugar

Salt and pepper

1 tbsp chopped curly parsley for garnish

Melt the butter in a heavy saucepan, add the chopped vegetables and cook until they begin to brown. Stir in the laver purée (laverbread) and the stock, bring to the boil and simmer until the vegetables are tender, about 25-30 minutes. Cool slightly, and then liquidise. Return to the saucepan, add the sugar and seasoning to taste. Bring to simmering point. Pour into bowls and garnish with the parsley. Serve with warm crusty bread.

Avocado, edamame bean and dulse bruschetta

Dulse Soup

The flavour in this simple soup comes from the dulse. It never ceases to confuse guests. Some think that it tastes meaty. When time permits, simmer the soup for longer to intensify the flavour of the wine-red dulse, which becomes green when cooked. Frozen dulse will defrost quickly, and if using dried dulse, reduce the quantity to 2 level tablespoons.

Ingredients (serves 2-3):
3 handfuls fresh dulse, finely chopped
15 g butter
1 tbsp oil
1 onion, peeled and finely chopped
2 medium potatoes peeled and bite-size diced
2 carrots, peeled small dice
750 ml dulse stock (2 tsps of dried dulse stirred into boiling water)

Put the butter and oil in a pan to melt over a low heat. Add the onion and cook briefly before adding the potato and carrot. Sauté for 3-4 minutes and then add the chopped dulse. Add enough seaweed stock to cover the sea and root vegetables and bring slowly to the boil. Reduce the heat and simmer for a minimum of 25 minutes, or longer as the flavour deepens. This soup may be served as is, or blended in a food processor. Add additional seaweed stock as required after blending.

Sugar Kelp Hummus

This recipe may be adapted to use with fresh dulse or an alternative species of dried seaweed, wireweed works well. A tablespoon of seaweed peanut butter can be used in place of the tahini, and use tinned chickpeas if you are short of time. For green seaweed presentation, mix a tablespoon of extra virgin olive oil with a large pinch of dried sea lettuce, and drizzle it over the bowl of hummus.

Ingredients (makes a small bowl):
6-8 cm sprig of sugar kelp and 2 ½ tbsps dried sugar kelp
200 g chickpeas
1 tsp bicarbonate soda
Juice of a large lemon
2 tbsps light tahini
Small garlic clove finely chopped
1 tbsp water
1 tbsps Greek yoghurt

Put the chickpeas in a bowl, cover with water and leave for 24 hours. Drain and rinse the chickpeas well and put them in a pan with the length of sugar kelp frond and the bicarbonate soda. Add water to cover the chickpeas and bring the pan to the boil. Boil rapidly until the chickpeas are tender (as per manufacturer's instruction), which was 2 ½ hours in my case, and remove any scum with a slotted spoon. Leave the chickpeas to cool in the water and then drain and pat them dry in a paper towel to remove excess water. Some people may like to remove the outer skin, but it adds fibre.

Heat a frying pan and dry roast the chickpeas with the remaining tablespoon of dried sugar kelp over a very low heat for 10 minutes, stirring occasionally. Leave to cool.

Meanwhile mix the lemon juice, tahini and crushed garlic together with a tablespoon of cold water until creamy. Put the roasted chickpeas and kelp, and creamed tahini in a food processor and blend to a paste. Add Greek yoghurt (to the desired consistency) and blend until the hummus is thick and creamy. Transfer into a bowl and serve with crudités or seaweed crisps.

Red Lentil, Root and Sea Vegetable Soup (V)

Ingredients (serves 4, vegan):
2 heaped tsps ground dried dulse

1.2 litre water
2 tbsp olive oil
Medium red onion, finely chopped
Medium carrot, peeled and diced
100 g swede, peeled and diced
150 g lentils
2 handfuls fresh dulse (or two tbsps dried)
Extra dried dulse for seasoning

Stir the heaped teaspoons of dried dulse into 600 ml of boiling water and set aside. Heat the oil in a saucepan on the hob. Add the prepared onion, carrot and swede and sauté briefly. Add the lentils and fresh or dried dulse, stir well and then add the dulse water. Bring the pan to the boil. Lower the heat and pop a lid on the pan. Simmer for 25 minutes or until the lentils are soft. Check the liquid levels occasionally and add water as necessary, with extra dried dulse.

Blend the soup in a liquidiser and use the remaining water to dilute to the desired consistency. Return the pan to the hob, season if necessary with extra dried dulse, heat through and serve.

Sea Oak Tapenade

Fresh dulse or one of the *Ulva spp* could replace the sea oak in this recipe, but seaweeds which require longer cooking time should be dried first. Adapt the recipe to the dried seaweed of your choice. If the seaweed is rehydrated before use, less oil will be required, but I prefer the seaweed to reconstitute in the oil. I sometimes add a teaspoon of pickled wild garlic buds, but this requires care or the tapenade is quickly over powered by garlic.

Ingredients (makes a small jar):
1 tbsp dried sea oak (to taste)
100 g black olives

2 anchovy fillets roughly chopped

1 tbsp capers, pickled wild garlic buds or pickled sea aster buds well drained

Juice half small lemon

Extra virgin olive oil

Put the sea oak, olives, anchovies and capers in a blender and roughly chop the ingredients. Add the lemon juice and enough olive oil to reach desired consistency. Spoon into a small jar and refrigerate. Tapenade can be used on canapés, added to sauces, stews and marinades, and used in stuffings.

Split Pea and Sugar Kelp Soup

When you poach a gammon joint in sugar kelp you are left with a delicious, gelatinous brown stock, which is perfect for a risotto or a soup. It marries well with split peas in a thick, warming soup.

Ingredients (serves 4):

Small 4-5 cm piece of sugar kelp

1 litre gammon and sugar kelp stock, fat skimmed

20 g butter

1 large leek, washed, finely diced

1 large carrot, peeled and diced

200 g split peas, rinsed and well drained

100 ml water

100 ml milk

Melt the butter in a large pan and sauté the leek and carrot for 2-3 minutes. Add the rinsed peas to the pan and stir briefly, to coat with butter. Add the sugar kelp frond and stock. Bring to the boil, cover and simmer over a low heat for 2-2 ½ hours until the peas are soft. Blend the soup in a food processor, adding water and milk until you reach the desired consistency. Return to the pan to heat through and serve.

Taramasalata

Some people soak the roe for an hour before using it, but I have found that this makes little difference to the overall taste. I often freeze roe; so perhaps using defrosted roe has the same effect. Add sea lettuce in place of bladder wrack for colour, but for my palate, the bladder wrack works superbly with the roe.

Ingredients (makes a small bowl):
1 heaped tsp dried bladder wrack, finely ground
10 cm (approx) piece cod roe
3 tbsps crème fraiche
Lime juice

Remove the skin and membrane from the cod roe and roughly chop, before putting it into a food processor. Add the crème fraiche and bladder wrack, and process briefly. Add lime juice to taste, blend and put into a small serving dish.

Wild Orache and Sea Rocket Soup

Orache and sea rocket are in season together and grow in close proximity. This often bodes well for a successful recipe. The dark green orache contrasts with the mauve flecks of sea rocket in this colourful soup.

Ingredients (serves 4):
450 g orache leaves, well washed and sand free
Scant tbsp sea rocket flowers, petals segmented, rinsed and dried (sand free)
4 sea rocket flowers (for decoration)

1 litre seaweed stock
25 g butter
1 tbsp oil
Banana shallot peeled and roughly diced
Large potato, peeled and diced into small pieces
Black pepper
2 tsps crème fraiche

Melt the butter and oil in a pan over a low heat and sauté the shallot and potato for 3-4 minutes, stirring continuously. Do not brown. Add half of the seaweed stock and bring to the boil. Lower the heat, cover and simmer for 10-12 minutes or until the potato begins to soften.

Add the orache and cook for 1-2 minutes to wilt. Season to taste and blend in a liquidiser or use a hand whisk. Return the soup to the pan and add enough stock to reach desired consistency. Add the sea rocket flowers and cook to heat through. Serve immediately with ½ teaspoon of crème fraiche decorated with a sea rocket petal in each bowl.

MAIN COURSES:
SEA & ROOT VEGETABLES

ROOT AND SEA VEGETABLE SALAD
This is perfect for early spring. It combines the earthy texture of winter's celeriac with new growth sea spaghetti

Ingredients: Serves 4
400 g fresh sea spaghetti
450 g celeriac
Large carrot

Juice half a small lemon

For the dressing
2 tsps finely grated fresh ginger
2 tbsps rice vinegar
Black pepper (few twists)
2 tbsps toasted sesame seeds
4 tbsps Greek Yoghurt
4 tbsps olive oil

Cut the sea spaghetti into fork-easy lengths. Pop half of the sea spaghetti into a colander and pour over a kettle of boiling water. It will turn green. Set aside to cool.

Peel the celeriac and cut it into thin, match sized pieces. No bigger. This is hard work – use a food processor if you are time short. Put the celeriac strips in a bowl, add the lemon juice and toss to coat (to prevent discolouration). Cut the carrot in a similar fashion and add to the prepared celeriac.

To make the dressing: Blend the rice vinegar, black pepper, sesame seeds and yoghurt together with the grated ginger. Whisk in the oil and pour over the prepared root vegetables. Toss well, season and add the green (blanched) and brown (raw) sea vegetables. Lightly mix the sea and root vegetables together and leave for ten minutes before serving.

DABBERLOCKS AND LIME INFUSED HALLOUMI
WITH TOMATO AND BEAN SALAD

Halloumi is a Cypriot cheese which cooks without losing its shape and absorbs flavour well. Halloumi is also delicious served in a seaweed batter. This recipe can be adapted to use kelp or dulse.

Ingredients (serves 4):
2 tbsp dried dabberlocks in 2 cm lengths (not ground)

3 tsps finely ground dried dabberlocks
1 nori sheet

For the marinade:
Juice and zest lime, well scrubbed
6 tbsps olive oil

For the salad:
250g halloumi
400 g broad beans
4 ripe large tomatoes

For the dressing:
2 tbsps rice wine vinegar
2 tbsps extra virgin olive oil
2tbsp light vegetable oil
1tsp sugar (to taste)
Freshly ground black pepper

Mix the marinade ingredients (lime juice, zest, olive oil and 2 teaspoons of dried dabberlocks) together in a shallow dish. Slice the halloumi into eight pieces and put them in the marinade. Baste well, cover and leave for as long as possible to allow the flavours to infuse. Turn the halloumi slices occasionally.

Cook the broad beans until just tender. Rinse in cold water to refresh, and drain well. If you are using older beans, nick the outer shell and remove. (Out of season, frozen beans work equally well.) Put the lengths of dabberlocks into a bowl and cover with cold water. Leave to soak for 5 minutes until softened. Put the dabberlocks in a small pan of boiling water and cook for 5 minutes or until tender – al dente. Drain and put the dabberlocks into the salad bowl. Plunge the tomatoes in boiling water for 10 seconds and then in cold water to remove the skins with ease, and then roughly chop the tomatoes. In a bowl, mix the beans with the diced tomatoes, sprinkle with the remaining teaspoon of dried dabberlocks and turn into a colander to drain.

Meanwhile, heat a griddle plate or grill until it is very hot and cook the halloumi slices on both sides until brown. Grill the nori sheet on each side for a few seconds under a hot grill – it burns quickly, so watch with care. (Or toast the nori over a gas flame.)

Whisk the dressing ingredients into the salad bowl with the prepared dabberlocks and add the well-drained broad beans and tomatoes. Lightly mix together and season to taste. Just before serving crumble the toasted nori over the salad. Serve the dabberlocks and lime halloumi warm, on the broad bean, dabberlocks and tomato salad. You may prefer to dice the cooked halloumi and add it to the salad bowl for a buffet style salad.

GOAT CHEESE COOKED IN MERMAID'S HAIR

Use frozen goat's cheese as it is easier to work with and choose a strongly-scented seaweed. Goat cheese may overpower kelp but pepper dulse will work well.

Ingredients (makes 4):
2 ½ tsps gutweed (or preferred dried seaweed)
2 slices of bread made into crumbs
75 g goats cheese (frozen)
2 tbsps sifted plain flour
Large egg lightly beaten

Preheat a deep fat fryer to 180 °C or manufacturer's suggested temperature. Mix the breadcrumbs and seaweed together in a shallow dish and put the flour and beaten egg into small bowls. Cut the defrosting cheese into 4 and dip each slice into flour and then egg, and then thickly coat it with the seaweed breadcrumbs. Place the coated slices on a tray and refrigerate for at least 10 minutes. Deep fat fry the slices individually for about 2 minutes (to manufacturer's instruction) until golden. Keep the cooked slices warm while cooking the remainder. Serve warm with a selection of beach salad leaves.

SEA AND ROOT VEGETABLE RISSOLES

Rissoles were one of my childhood favourites and they are a good way to use up leftovers. The name is said to have originated from the Latin for red, so it seems appropriate to use red seaweed, even if it turns green when cooked.

Ingredients (makes 6):
Small frond dulse and 50 g fresh dulse coarsely chopped
200 g celeriac
300 g parsnips
3 tbsp oil
15 g butter
1 tsp coriander seeds ground
½ tsp cumin
½ tsp mustard seeds
Oil for frying

Set the oven to 180 ºC / Gas 4. Peel and chop the celeriac into small, evenly sized cubes, then parboil it with the dulse frond in a pan of boiling water for 2-3 minutes. Drain well and remove the dulse frond and pat dry with kitchen roll. Meanwhile peel and chop the parsnips into evenly sized pieces. Put the oil and butter into an ovenproof dish, add the spices and heat in the preheated oven for 3-4 minutes. Add the prepared root and coarsely chopped sea vegetables to the dish, and toss well to coat with oil. Cover and bake for 45-50 minutes or until the vegetables are soft.

Turn the cooked vegetables into a bowl. Add enough of the juices to easily mash with a potato masher and leave to cool. Mould 6 rissoles and refrigerate until firm. Heat a little oil in a frying pan and fry the sea and root rissoles for 3-4 minutes on each side, until golden and heated through.

SEA SCENTED AND ROASTED PEPPERS

This easily prepared supper or lunch dish is delicious served with a simple salad and seaweed sourdough. The anchovies, olives and sea lettuce could be replaced by a heaped teaspoon of sea oak tapenade (see recipe on page 160).

Ingredients (makes 8):
4 tsps finely ground dried gutweed or sea lettuce (Ulva spp)
4 large red peppers, washed and dried
8 large tomatoes
24 black olives, pitted
8 scant tbsps olive oil
16 anchovies

Set the oven to 190 °C / Gas 5. Cut the peppers in half, leaving the stalk intact, and remove the seeds. Lay the pepper halves skin side down on an ovenproof baking dish, and sprinkle half a teaspoon of finely ground seaweed into the empty cavity of each pepper. Plunge the tomatoes in a bowl of boiling water for 10-15 seconds, depending on freshness, then refresh in cold water and peel off the skins. Put the tomatoes into a bowl, roughly chop and divide the mixture between the peppers.

Push 3 olives into each pepper half and pour a scant tablespoon of olive oil over the top. Scatter the remaining dried seaweed over the peppers and bake in a preheated oven for about 40 minutes until the peppers are soft. Remove from the oven and crisscross two anchovies over each pepper. Place under a preheated grill for 2-3 minutes to heat the anchovies and serve immediately.

Sea Spaghetti and Chorizo Risotto

Sea spaghetti is at its best when young (in early spring). I add roughly 100 g of chopped seaweed to the final minutes of a risotto cooking time. It adds colour, flavour and texture. Use your favourite recipes and add the chopped sea spaghetti for the final 3-4 minutes of cooking time. The brown seaweed will turn green.

Ingredients (serves 4):

50 g butter

1 tbsp olive oil

Half small leek, finely chopped

300 g risotto rice

900 ml warm dulse stock (2 tsps dried dulse stirred into the warm water)

75 g chorizo diced

100 g sea spaghetti, rinsed and roughly chopped

50 g frozen peas

Black pepper

2 tbsps cream cheese

Heat the butter in a large shallow pan over a low heat and sauté the leeks for 1-2 minutes. Add the rice and continue to cook, stirring to gloss the rice grains. Do not allow to brown. Add the warm stock, a little at a time. When the rice is almost soft (has absorbed the stock) add the chorizo, sea spaghetti and frozen peas. Season well. Stir over a low heat for a further 2-3 minutes until the brown sea spaghetti turns green. Add the cream cheese, stir to combine and serve.

Spring Root and Sea Vegetable Frittatas

Frittatas are delicious hot or cold for picnics. Spring brings the first Jersey potatoes and lore suggests it is the time when seaweed is at its most nutritious. Seawater, which has been strained to remove impurities, is ideal for boiling vegetables and steaming fish.

Ingredients (makes 12):
3 tbsps finely chopped fresh dulse or sugar kelp or 2 tbsps fresh sea lettuce
Butter for greasing
250 g scrubbed new potatoes as small as possible
6 large eggs
150 ml milk
Pinch Cayenne pepper
Seawater, strained through muslin
Oil for greasing

Set the oven to 200 °C / Gas 6. Lightly oil a muffin tray. Steam or boil the potatoes in seawater until they are just soft. When the potatoes are cool enough to handle, cut them into small, evenly sized chunks and divide them between the muffin moulds. Break the eggs into a bowl and lightly whisk. Then whisk in the milk and season with cayenne pepper. Divide the finely chopped fresh sea vegetables between the moulds and pour the egg and milk mix equally over the top. Put the tray into the preheated oven and bake for 10-12 minutes or until the frittata is just set. (To test that the frittata has set insert a cocktail stick – it should come out clean.) Allow the frittatas to cool briefly and then loosen each frittata with a palette knife before turning them out.

ROCKET AND DULSE PESTO

This infuses the umami of the fresh sea vegetable, dulse, with that of rocket. In the warmer months wild rocket can be gathered throughout Britain. Finely chopped and dried laver also compliments rocket, but if you make this, increase the quantities of lemon juice and oil accordingly. Seaweed may be added to flavour homemade pasta too. Dulse pesto mixed with breadcrumbs can be coated on a leg or rack of lamb prior to cooking – another umami.

Ingredients (makes a small jar):
3 tbsp fresh dulse finely chopped
25 g Parmesan
40 g rocket
Small clove, garlic finely chopped
100 ml extra virgin olive oil
Juice small lemon
Freshly ground pepper, few twists

Put all of the ingredients apart from the oil, lemon juice and pepper into a food processor and blend well. Add enough oil to make a thick paste and then season with lemon juice and pepper to taste. Put the pesto into a small bowl, cover and refrigerate for up to 10 days (or freeze). Dulse pesto can be served with pasta, poultry, or fish parcels, on canapés, or in soups.

TOMATO, PEPPER AND KNOTTED WRACK TART

The knotted wrack *Ascsophyllum nodosum* thickens the tomato sauce and adds a hint of the sea to both the tomato sauce and the flaky pastry tart crust. This tart is equally delicious hot or cold.

Ingredients (serves 6):
2 tbsps olive oil
1 small onion, finely chopped
1 stick celery, finely chopped
3 tsps dried Ascophyllum nodosum, finely ground
400 g tin chopped tomatoes
1 brightly coloured pepper
250 g cherry tomatoes (about 15)
1tbsp toasted pine nuts

171

Wholemeal flour
425 g puff pastry

Oven 200 ºC / Gas 7 (Fan). Add one tablespoon of olive oil to a saucepan and cook over a moderate heat. Add the chopped onion and celery and sauté briefly. Add 2 teaspoons of *Ascophyllum nodosum*, stir well and add the tomatoes. Cook for 5-6 minutes until the sauce has thickened and the vegetables are beginning to soften.

Meanwhile cut the pepper in half and remove the seeds and stalk. Place the pepper halves, skin side up under a hot grill to brown. Pop the peppers in a plastic bag for 5 minutes, and then remove the skins. Thinly slice the peppers and set aside.

Use the remaining olive oil to grease a 24 x 24 cm shallow ovenproof dish. Scatter the cherry tomatoes, toasted pine nuts and sliced pepper over the base of the dish. Tip the tomato sauce over the vegetables.

Lightly dust a work surface with with flour and roll the pastry out to roughly fit the dish. Pop it over the prepared vegetables and tuck the edges under, to fit.

Bake the tart in a pre set oven for 20-25 minutes until the pastry is golden brown. Leave the tart to cool for 2-3 minutes and then hold a serving plate over the top of the tart and flip the contents onto the serving plate.

MAIN COURSES: FISH

COCKLES AND MUSSELS STEAMED OVER SEAWEED SERVED IN A BEACH WRAP

This can also be cooked on a seashore barbeque, if the sauce is prepared earlier and kept warm in a flask or reheated in a pan on a barbecue. A wrack is ideal because this is the first species that you come across as you walk down to the beach. Cook the shellfish as suggested using foraged seaweed and top up the pan with seawater. Wrap the tortilla wraps in foil and heat them in fading embers (towards the edge of the fires, where the coals are less fierce). Beach barbeques lend themselves to foil wrapped fish parcels. Try bladder wrack and mackerel or salmon liberally spread with sea lettuce butter.

Ingredients (serves 4):
½ carrier bag of any wrack, but well rinsed bladder wrack is ideal
Seawater
2 kg cockles or mussels
2 limes quartered

Cover the base of a deep frying pan with seaweed. Add water to cover the seaweed. Bring the water to the boil and when it begins to steam, add mussels or cockles and the limes and cover with silver foil. Remove the foil after 3-4 minutes to see if the shells have opened. Remove the cooked shellfish as they open. Discard any shells that fail to open. If using a small pan, cook the shellfish in batches. Cooked cockles and mussels are also delicious served in the following sauce:

Tomato and Bladder wrack Sauce

This tomato sauce recipe stands alone without the mussel juices. My friend Dr Duncan Smallman of Slate Island Seaweed uses a similar tomato and seaweed sauce recipe. He adds three mushrooms (wild, if you are a competent forager) and replaces the dried bladder wrack with 15 g of fresh dulse. If using fresh seaweed the sauce would benefit from emulsifying.

Ingredients (serves 4):
2 ½ tsps dried ground bladder wrack
1 tbsp oil
Knob butter

1 red onion, peeled, finely diced
2 sticks celery, finely chopped
500 g passata
8 cherry tomatoes
1 tsp lime juice
Black pepper

Heat the oil and butter in a frying pan and cook the onion for 2-3 minutes. Add the bladder wrack and celery and cook briefly. Pour in the passata and cherry tomatoes and bring the pan to the boil, cover and simmer for 12-15 minutes. Boil rapidly to reduce (thicken) the tomato sauce. Adjust the seasoning. Add any cockle (or mussel) juices to the thickened tomato sauce with lime juice to taste. Stir well and heat to reduce slightly (if there is a lot of cockle juice). Add the cooked cockles (or mussels) and cook to heat through.

To make beach wraps: warm tortilla wraps as per manufacturer's instruction and fill with the rich, tomato sauce, shellfish and roughly chopped foraged beach salad leaves.

CRAB PANNA COTTA
Crab in a creamy set, with seaweed from the lower seashore.

Ingredients (makes 4-6 depending on size):
20 g carrageen (rehydrated)
Heaped tsp ground gutweed or sea lettuce to taste
4-5 crab claws (175 g crab meat)
250 ml milk
250 ml double cream
1 tsp lime zest

Heat the milk and carrageen for about 15 minutes until it is thick and gelatinous. Strain the milk through a nylon sieve to leave around 100 ml of thick liquid. Put the double cream in a pan with the carrageen milk and heat to just below boiling point. Add the lime zest, gutweed or sea lettuce (to taste) and crab, stir briefly and pour into moulds. Leave to cool and refrigerate until use. To serve: briefly dip the mould in hot water, loosen the set crab with a knife and turn onto a serving plate.

KELP POACHED SALMON, LAVER AND SEVILLE ORANGE EN CROUTE

A recipe inspired by Dorothy Hartley. Testing the recipe in January allowed me to use Seville orange juice in this glossy laver sauce, but out of season replace the bitter orange with a lemon. A heaped teaspoon of pomegranate seeds will add texture and colour too.

Ingredients (makes 4):
6 cm sugar kelp frond 8 tbsps prepared laverbread
4 x100 g salmon fillets
400 g puff pasty
4 heaped tsps marmalade
Juice and zest half Seville orange (or lemon)
15 g butter
Extra flour
Egg-wash

Set the oven to 220 ºC / Gas 7. Fill a pan with enough water to cover 4 salmon fillets. Add the sugar kelp and bring the water to the boil. Simmer for 20 minutes to allow the kelp to infuse into the water. Remove the pan from the heat and put the salmon fillets into the hot kelp water. Put a lid on the pan and set aside for about 30-40 minutes until the salmon is almost poached. Use a slotted spoon to remove the fillets from the pan onto a plate and leave to cool.

Lightly dust a surface with flour and roll 4 rectangles approx 18 cm x 10 cm (to wrap the salmon in). Place a tablespoon of laverbread (cooked laver) off centre towards the front of the pastry (to cover the salmon fillet but leaving the ends free) and place the well drained poached salmon on top of the laver. Spread a teaspoon of marmalade on the salmon, and egg-wash the sides of the pastry. Fold the nearest side of the pastry over the salmon to make a parcel and press and crimp the edges to seal. Brush the parcel with egg-wash and pierce the top to allow steam to escape. Bake for 12-15 minutes in a preheated oven until golden.

Meanwhile in a saucepan, heat the remaining laverbread, butter, Seville zest and juice together, whisking well to make a thick and glossy sauce to serve with the salmon.

Potted Seaside Shrimps

The perfect bread to toast and serve potted shrimps on is seaweed sourdough, but if you are packing a picnic, oatcakes or crisp breads work too. Potted shrimps are traditionally flavoured with nutmeg and mace, but sea lettuce adds colour and is a reminder of provenance.

Ingredients (makes 12 mini muffin cases for a picnic):
1 ½ tsps finely ground sea lettuce (to taste)
200 g unsalted butter
1 tsp lemon juice
250 g cooked shrimps

Melt the butter over a low heat until there are small dark flecks, and then strain it through a sieve lined with muslin into a jug. Return the butter to a clean pan and add the sea lettuce and lemon juice and simmer for 5 minutes. Leave to cool but not set.

Divide the shrimps between the silicone muffin cases, packing them as tightly as possible. Divide the sea lettuce butter between the moulds and refrigerate until set.

Sugar Kelp and Scallop Omelette

This simple supper begs a glass of white wine but little else.

Ingredients:
25 g fresh sugar kelp finely chopped
2 large eggs
Black pepper
Knob butter
1 scallop very finely sliced

Cook the sugar kelp in boiling water for 5 minutes and drain well. Break the eggs into a bowl, whisk briefly and season with black pepper. Heat a 20 cm omelette pan and add a knob of butter. When the butter foams add the beaten eggs and cook until the base begins to set. Scatter the sugar kelp and scallop over the egg and continue cooking until the egg sets. Increase the heat to lightly brown the base. Fold the omelette in half, remove the pan from the heat and transfer the omelette to a warm plate.

Smoked Seaweed Cockles

I cajoled the assistance of the Isle of South Uist's doctor, Stephen Bird in this task. After minor disagreement concerning pairing of food with stand-alone dried seaweed or seaweed combined with conventional wood chippings, seaweed won the day. The smoked cockles taste distinctive – umami.

Ingredients (makes a dozen):
2 tbsps dried seaweed (of choice)
Smoker (a stovetop mini smoker)
Foil (to aid cleaning)
12 evenly sized clean cockles

Line the stovetop smoker with silver foil and sprinkle the finely ground dried seaweed in a circle to correspond with the size of the largest hob/gas ring. Heat over a moderate heat and place the well-washed cockles on the rack. The cockles will dry smoke to begin with. As the first wisp of smoke appears, close the lid and start the cooking time. Maintain the heat for 15-20 minutes. It is important to ensure that the lid seals properly. The juice from the opening shellfish will turn this into a wet smoke, which is both clever and delicious. The exact size and amount of cockles will dictate precise smoking time. To avoid too much smoke in the kitchen, carefully take the smoker outside before opening. We like to eat the cockles straight from the shells but you could serve them in a tomato sauce with pasta or on toast.

RAZOR CLAM CEVICHE

It is easy to overcook razor clams and this delicious ceviche avoids the problem. Freeze the clams for a few hours to make the meat easier to remove from the shells. It tenderises it too. The sea lettuce may be replaced with a tablespoon of finely chopped Scots lovage.

Ingredients (serves 4):
2 tsps dried finely ground sea lettuce
12 razor clams stomach discarded, thinly sliced
2 grapefruit segments roughly diced, juice reserved
2 tbsps olive oil
2 tsps caster sugar

Dry roast the sea lettuce in a pan and leave to cool. In a bowl mix the grapefruit segments, juice, oil and sugar together and stir in the seaweed. Add the finely sliced razor clams and gently stir together well. Cover and refrigerate for at least two hours, stirring occasionally. Season and serve as an appetiser.

Sea spaghetti and scallop omelette

White Fish in Spelt, Sea Lettuce and Ale Batter

I find that batter stays crispier after frying if I use a yeast batter. A spelt batter is however quite heavy, so I've mixed it with plain flour and added sea lettuce, beer and yeast – the flavour is delicious. The batter could also be used to coat halloumi cheese.

Ingredients (serves 4):
1 heaped tsp dried sea lettuce (to taste)
175 g plain flour
50 g spelt
7 g dried yeast (sachet)
Pinch sugar
300 ml ale
4 white fish fillets (175 g)
Seasoned flour to coat fish fillets

Sift the dry ingredients (plain flour and spelt, then add the yeast, sugar and dried sea lettuce) into a bowl. Stir and make a well in the centre and slowly whisk the ale into the mixture to make a smooth, thick batter. Cover and leave at room temperature for an hour. Stir the batter well before using.

Cook the fish fillets one by one: dip in seasoned flour (to remove moisture from the fish), shake well to remove surplus flour and then dip in the prepared batter. Fry in a hot deep fat fryer (160 °C) for 4-5 minutes or to manufacturer's instruction until crispy and golden. Turn on to kitchen paper to remove excess oil. Keep the fish warm while you cook the remaining fillets.

White Fish and Dulse on Toast

I think that dulse tastes smoky, but the more ambitious might like to use white fish which has been smoked over seaweed for a more intense smoked flavour. Smoked cockles (see recipe on page 177) would also be delicious in this simple variation of Welsh Rarebit.

Ingredients (serves 4):
10 cm dulse frond and 2 heaped tbsp fresh dulse, finely chopped
150 ml milk
150 ml water
225 g fillets white fish
50 g butter
50 g plain flour
50 g mature cheddar, finely grated
Large egg yolk
Splash lemon juice
Black pepper
4 thick slices of sourdough (ideally seaweed)

In a pan heat the milk, water and dulse frond to boiling point and remove from the stove. Put the fish fillets in the pan, cover with a lid and leave to cool, to allow the flavour to infuse. Return the pan to the stove and poach the fish over a low heat until it is cooked. Remove the fish with a fish slice or slotted spoon and reserve the poaching liquid. Discard the dulse and when cool, flake the fish into a bowl. Heat the butter in a pan and beat in the flour to make a roux (paste). Slowly whisk in the reserved poaching stock and the finely chopped dulse, stirring continuously (to avoid lumps) as the sauce thickens. Cook for 5 minutes and then stir in the cheese to melt and remove from the stove. Transfer the sauce into a bowl and beat in the egg yolk. Add the lemon juice and flaked fish and season with black pepper.

To serve: Preheat a grill and lightly toast the slices of sourdough on both sides. Divide the fish and dulse mixture between the bread and place under a preheated grill until it is golden.

MAIN COURSES: MEAT

BEEF CHEEK AND SEAWEED CASSEROLE

Kelp adds flavour without the necessity for beef or vegetable stock, and carrageen adds thickness and sheen. Laver dumplings are delicious served with casseroled beef cheeks. Replace the beef with venison or lamb if you prefer.

Ingredients (serves 6):
100 g kelp fronds roughly chopped, 2 tbsps carrageen gel (see page 45)
2 tbsps oil
2 beef cheeks
1 onion, finely sliced
½ red onion, finely sliced
300 g carrots, peeled, chopped on the diagonal in large slices
2 sticks celery, washed, diagonally sliced
Freshly ground black pepper
Water or seaweed stock

Heat a heavy-based casserole dish and add the oil. Seal the beef cheeks in the hot oil and transfer to a plate. Add the kelp and remaining additional ingredients. Stir briefly for 2 minutes to coat the vegetables in oil. Return the beef cheeks to the pan and fill with water or seaweed stock to cover the beef and vegetables. Bring the pan to the boil and simmer for 3-4 hours until the beef falls away when forked. Add the carrageen gel for the final 30 minutes of cooking time, and stir well. Check liquid levels occasionally during cooking and replenish as necessary. Season to taste and serve with laver dumplings, rice, pasta or potatoes.

BLADDER WRACK SEAWEED SKIRLIE

Skirlie, also known as Poor Man's Haggis, is a versatile Scottish dish that encourages meat frugality. When steamed it is known as Mealie Pudding. Vegetarians may replace the suet with olive oil and it will be less calorie dense. However, for flavour, suet and seaweed marry well. The Scots cook F. Marian McNeill used suet, but butter or dripping also work well. Skirlie traditionally accompanied chicken or game. It can be used in stuffing or as a crust for meat or fish before oven baking. Use it as a base for soup, in a savoury crumble topping, or mixed into mashed root vegetables. Some eat Skirlie on toast, others enjoy it on top of a Scotch pie. It's a traditional recipe that is making a comeback.

Ingredients (serves 4-6):

50 g grated suet or lard (or a butter and lard combination)

Medium onion, finely chopped

1 or 2 tbsps dried seaweed, depending on species (e.g. 2 tbsps dried laver)

Approx 175 g pinhead oatmeal

Melt the fat slowly in a heavy based pan. Add the chopped onion and seaweed. Cook over a low heat, stirring well until the onion softens. Add enough oatmeal to absorb the fat. Cook for 30-40 minutes until the oatmeal softens. If you use medium oatmeal, the process will be speedier. Season with salt and black pepper. This recipe lends itself to long, slow oven cooking – ideally use a cast iron casserole dish with a lid.

Gammon Poached and Roasted in Sugar Kelp

One would expect seaweed and gammon to be a salty combination but the mannitol in the sugar kelp adds a subtle sweetness and the resulting brown poaching stock is delicious, not in the least saline.

Ingredients:

Large frond sugar kelp (30 cm), halved

2 kg gammon boneless joint

For the glaze
1-2 tbsp soft brown sugar

Set the oven to 200 ºC / Gas 6 (after poaching time). Use string to loosely tie the sugar kelp fronds around the gammon and put it in a large pan. Fill the pan with water to cover the joint. Bring the water to the boil, cover and then simmer for about 1 ½ – 2 hours until a meat thermometer reaches 65-70 ºC when pushed into the centre of the gammon. Remove the gammon from the water and leave to cool for 10 minutes. Unwrap the sugar kelp and carefully remove the gammon skin without removing the fat. Rub the brown sugar onto the fat. Use the cooked sugar kelp fronds to encase and protect the cooked gammon. Cover the sugar kelp with foil, leaving the glaze exposed. Bake in a preheated oven for 10 minutes or until the glaze is golden. Carve when the gammon is cold.

LA–SEA-AGNE

I was wandering along the beach and spied six stormcast sugar kelp fronds still attached to a large pebble. The crinkly fronds reminded me of pasta. This dish is packed with sea vegetable flavour – no additional seasoning is required. I must thank Silvana de Soissons for the name of this recipe.

Ingredients (serves 4-6):
6 fresh sugar kelp fronds (20-25 cm).
1½ tsps pepper dried dulse
25 g butter
1 tbsp olive oil
Large leek, trimmed and finely chopped
400 g tin tomatoes
50 ml water

Sea spaghetti lasagne

500 g lamb mince
15 g plain flour
300 ml milk
25 g finely grated cheese

Set the oven to 180 ºC / Gas 4. Melt 15 g butter and the olive oil in a pan. Add the chopped leeks and sauté for 3-4 minutes without colouring the leeks. Add the tomatoes, 50 ml water and a teaspoon of dried pepper dulse. Bring to the boil and simmer for 10 minutes until the sauce is thick. Brown the mince in a frying pan and drain off excess fat. Melt the remaining butter in a pan and add the flour. Cook for 2-3 minutes stirring with a wooden spoon until the roux leaves the sides of the pan clean. Slowly add the milk stirring continuously until the sauce thickens. Add the remaining scant half teaspoon of pepper dulse and cook for 2-3 minutes. Cover to prevent a skim from forming. Heat a pan with boiling water and cook the sugar kelp fronds for 4-5 minutes. They will turn green.

Assemble the La-sea-agne in a medium-sized ovenproof dish, layering the mince, tomato sauce, and sugar kelp, and finishing with a layer of white sauce. Scatter the cheese over the top and bake for 30-35 minutes until golden in a preheated oven.

ORIENTAL STYLE PORK RIB AND SEAWEED BROTH

Catherine Phipps created this delicious recipe, which is cooked in a pressure cooker.

Ingredients (serves 4):
15 g dried kombu or wakame
1 tbsp vegetable oil
500-750g pork spare ribs
3 garlic cloves, finely chopped
2 ½ cm piece ginger, grated
3 cm piece cinnamon stick
½ a star anise
1 tsp Szechuan pepper
1 chilli (optional)
1 litre chicken or pork stock

To serve
1 tbsp light soy sauce
1 tsp rice or cider vinegar
1 head of broccoli, broken into florets
100 g shitake mushrooms, sliced
4 spring onions, cut into lengths and shredded
Noodles or rice

Soak the seaweed in water for a few minutes until soft. Shred finely and set aside. Heat the oil in the base of the pressure cooker. When it is hot, add the spare ribs and brown thoroughly. Add the garlic, ginger and spices then sprinkle in the chopped seaweed and stock. Fix on the lid, bring to high pressure and cook for 30 minutes. Allow the pressure to drop naturally. Open the lid. Add the soy sauce, vinegar, broccoli and mushrooms. Bring to high pressure again and release pressure immediately, fast. The broccoli should be just al dente. Taste for seasoning and add salt and more soy sauce if necessary. Serve with steamed rice or noodles and garnish with the spring onions.

WELSH LAVERBREAD, COCKLE AND BACON PIE

Elisabeth Luard kindly contributed this recipe. If you have foraged, dried and toasted laver you might like to add 2 tsps of finely ground laver to the potato pastry. Julia Horton-Powdrill who runs seaweed foraging courses in Pembrokeshire serves a similar pie at lunch, after her courses.

Ingredients (serves 3-4):
2 tbsps prepared laverbread
Potato pastry
100 g butter, chilled and diced
100 g self-raising flour
Pinch salt
150 g cold mashed potato

For the filling::
Scrap of butter
2 tbsps diced bacon
100 g prepared cockles or shucked mussels
300 ml single cream
4 egg yolks
Salt and paper
Flour to dust

Set the oven to 200 °C / Gas 6. Make the pastry. Rub the butter into the flour with the salt using the tips of your fingers. When the mixture looks like fine breadcrumbs, work in the potato and knead lightly until you have a smooth ball of dough. Lightly dust a work surface with flour and roll out the dough to line a buttered (20 cm) tart-tin – it won't need to rest. Prick with a fork, line with foil and weight with dried beans. Bake the pastry-case in the preheated oven for 10 minutes to set the pastry, then remove the lining and slip the case back into the oven for a few minutes for the surface to dry.

Meanwhile, fry the bacon gently in the butter till the fat runs. Add the shellfish and laver and stir over the heat for just long enough to heat the laver (don't let it boil). Whisk the cream with the egg yolks, stir in the contents of the pan and season with salt and pepper. When the pastry case has cooled a little, spoon in the filling. Return the tart to the oven, lower the heat to 190 °C / Gas 5, and bake for 35-40 minutes until lightly set and golden brown (it'll firm as it cools).

VEGETABLE ACCOMPANIMENTS

LAVER DUMPLINGS

Dumplings are comfort food at its best. This recipe can be adapted to use any finely ground, dried seaweed – simply replace the laver with extra water. Cooked laver may not look very appetising but the resulting dumplings are surprisingly colourful and packed with flavour. Add laver dumplings to a hearty stew and carbohydrates will take on a whole new dimension. A tablespoon of carrageen gel will enhance and give sheen to any stew or casserole. Cooked laver can also be added to potatoes or fish cakes.

Ingredients (makes 6-8 dumplings depending on size):
2 tbsps prepared laverbread
125 g self raising flour
50 g suet
1 tbsp water

Put the dry ingredients into a bowl and mix in the cooked laver. Add enough water to work to a firm dough. Divide the laver dough into six and roll into balls. Add the dumplings for the last 25-30 minutes of a stew cooking time.

Leeks and Carrots Braised in Kelp and Verjuice

On the Isle of South Uist I rarely see the tiny leeks and green topped carrots of the mainland supermarket. I'm pushed to find verjuice too, but re-corked verjuice can be refrigerated for a month or so. I love the gentle acidity of verjuice, when citrus juice is too sharp. After a trip to the mainland I cross The Minch with plenty of tiny vegetables that hint of nouvelle cuisine, and then I marry them with dried Uist kelp.

Ingredients (serves 4 as a side salad)
12 tiny leeks
12 baby topped carrots
2 tbsps dried kelp
Sea salt
500 ml verjuice
Black Pepper

Pop leeks, carrots, kelp and sea salt into a pan with the verjuice. Cook over a low heat until the leeks are just tender and the carrots retain a slight bite. Remove the vegetables to a serving dish and boil the remaining liquid to reduce by half. Season with black pepper and pour the reduced verjuice over the cooked vegetables.

New Potatoes with Wings of Dabberlocks & Lemon

New potatoes herald the start of summer and early in the season (May and early June) I often cook them with young dabberlocks wings. It's a wonderful combination. The wings of dabberlocks are similar in taste to the vegetable mange tout.

Ingredients (serves 4):
500 g small new potatoes, scrubbed
12-15 young dabberlocks wings, halved
25 g butter
Zest half lemon
Freshly ground black pepper

Scrub the new potatoes. Cut any larger potatoes in half. Cook in a minimum of water for 15 minutes or until the potatoes are just soft. (Test with a knife.) Add the dabberlocks wings to the potatoes for the last five minutes of cooking time. Strain the vegetables.

Pop the butter and lemon zest into a bowl. Add the warm, cooked vegetables and toss well to coat in the butter and lemon. Turn into a warm serving dish and season with freshly ground black pepper.

SALADS

JAPANESE SEAWEED SALAD

A sweet, citrusy, fresh salad from Dr Alice Liu, who says that this recipe is easy to improvise and can be used both as a main meal or a side salad.

Ingredients:
100 g kelp (rehydrated if dried)
100 g grated cucumber, well drained
100 g grated carrot, well drained
Equal quantities of each of the following: sesame oil, mirin, soy sauce, miso, rice vinegar (or lemon juice), sesame seeds. Begin with 2 tsps of each and add more if required to dress the salad

1 tsp honey (optional)
½ tsp finely chopped chilli (optional)

Mix everything together and season to taste.

SEASIDE SALAD

Ingredients (serves 4):
400 g sea spaghetti
4 eggs, hard boiled
½ cucumber deseeded, bite sized chopped
2 handfuls chopped fennel
2 large ripe tomatoes, chopped
3 tbsps extra virgin olive oil
Juice half a lime
Freshly ground pepper

Cook the sea spaghetti in boiling water for 3-4 minutes (longer, later in the season). Drain and refresh in cold water. Shake well to remove excess water. Pop the seaweed into a bowl and add the eggs and prepared terrestrial vegetables. Mix the vinaigrette in a small jug and pour it over the salad. Season and lightly toss the ingredients together. Decant the salad into a serving dish and serve.

SEA SPAGHETTI SLAW

This recipe was created by my daughter in law, Elizabeth, after she had dined on seaweed coleslaw in a London restaurant.

Ingredients (serves 4)
15 g dried sea spaghetti
2 small pak choi

¼ red cabbage
½ large carrot
1 ½ tbsp sesame oil
2 tsp rice vinegar
Toasted sesame seeds to garnish

Simmer the sea spaghetti as per the instructions on the packet. Meanwhile, finely shred the red cabbage and the stems of the pak choi. Grate the carrot with a large hole grater.

Once the sea spaghetti is cooked, drain and refill the pan with cold water to cool the spaghetti down. Add in an icecube if you're in a rush! Toast the sesame seeds in a dry frying pan until they turn a golden brown.

Drain the cold water off the sea spaghetti, combine all the ingredients in a large bowl and mix thoroughly.

This goes particularly well with Chinese-style pork burgers (pork, sesame seeds, spring onions, soy sauce), but would work wherever you normally have coleslaw. In season use fresh sea spaghetti.

CHINESE KELP AND TOFU SALAD

Dr Alice Liu says that this salad is more vinegary and spicy than her recipe for Japanese Seaweed Salad (see page 190).

Ingredients:
2 handfuls kelp (rehydrated if dried)
150 g tofu, small dice
Equal quantities (2-3 tsps)of each ingredient below until you've enough to coat the kelp and tofu
Chinese black vinegar, soy sauce, sesame oil, chilli oil (preferably Sichuan).
Clove of minced garlic
Handful of finely chopped spring onion
Vegetable oil (optional as required)

Sea spaghetti slaw

Mix everything together and add salt, pepper and sugar to taste.

Some tips from Dr Alice: Pop silky tofu in the freezer. The freezing process changes its texture and makes it tougher, easier to cut and cook – and nicer in my opinion. The tofu becomes aerated and soaks up more sauce…it's something Chinese people do for hotpots and so on.

For crispy tofu: Cube and pan fry in a tablespoon of vegetable oil (coating it in sesame seeds is optional). Before pan frying, I press tofu lightly for a couple hours with a heavy chopping board and some kitchen towel to get rid of as much moisture as possible, without breaking it up. This makes the tofu more chewy.

Warm Brussel Sprout, Dulse and Chestnut Salad

Ingredients (serves 4):

2 tbsp vegetable oil

200 g Brussel sprouts, trimmed and very finely sliced or marinated in seaweed and oil, then par boiled for a richer flavour prior to frying

Half red onion, very thinly diced

50 g fresh dulse, washed and roughly chopped or 2 tbsps dried

25 g Micro-herbs or Alfalfa Sprouts

5 g poppy seeds

25 g Edamame beans, cooked

Lemon and olive oil for dressing

Sea salt and black pepper

Heat the oil and stir fry the sprouts, onion and dulse until the red onion begins to soften but retains its bite.

Add the micro-herbs, poppy seeds and Edamame beans and stir together briefly. Add a squeeze of lemon and olive oil to dress. Season to taste. You can vary the seaweed species and sea lettuce works well.

Warm brussel sprout, dulse and chestnut salad

WARM DULSE INFUSED QUINOA AND RED RICE SALAD

This salad is flavoured with dulse, a delicious red seaweed that some say tastes like bacon – no additional seasoning is required.

Ingredients (serves 2-3 as a main course):

150 g quinoa
150 g Camargue red rice
3 tbsps dulse, dried and finely ground
1 red pepper
1 orange pepper
2 small tomatoes, diced
2 avocado, diced
2 tbsps extra virgin olive oil
Juice half a small lemon
2 tbsps finely chopped parsley

Rinse the quinoa and put it in a saucepan with 1 tablespoon of the dried dulse and 450 ml water. Place the pan on the hob and bring to the boil. Lower the heat, cover and simmer for 20 minutes.

Meanwhile, pop the red rice into a pan and cover with 450 ml boiling water and 1 tablespoon of dried dulse. Cook for 25 minutes or until the rice is just tender. Drain the quinoa and red rice in the same colander. Mix together and rinse the grains briefly with boiling water. Return to a pan and stir in the remaining dulse. Cover with a lid and set aside.

Cut the peppers in half and remove the stalk and seeds. Soften the peppers under a medium grill for five minutes. Allow the peppers to cool briefly, coarsely dice and pop in a bowl with the chopped tomatoes and avocados. Add the vegetables, lemon juice, oil and parsley to the warm grains and season to taste. Eat as soon as possible.

DESSERTS: HOT

BAKED SEAWEED ALASKA

450 g leftover Christmas pudding
10 tablespoons soft ice-cream
4 large egg whites
250 g caster sugar
1 tbsp dried finely ground laver

Spoon two-thirds of the ice-cream to line a 2 pint jelly mould or pudding dish lined with cling film. Put the Christmas pudding in the centre, so that it is encased by ice-cream. Pop the remaining ice-cream on top to parcel the ice-cream. Freeze for an hour and then turn the frozen pudding out on to a freezer- and oven-safe platter. Return the pudding to the freezer.

Pre heat the oven 220 ºC / Gas 7. Meanwhile make the meringue. Make a cooked Italian meringue if you want to. Place the egg whites in a clean bowl and use an electric whisk to beat the whites until they form stiff peaks. Gradually whisk in the caster sugar and whisk until the mixture is stiff and glossy. Fold in the dried laver.

Remove the pudding from the freezer and work quickly to clad it in laver meringue. Cook the pudding for about five minutes in the preheated oven until the meringue is lightly browned and eat immediately.

OCEANUS NEMESIS

These individual sponge puddings ooze gooey chocolate and memories of the seashore. This pudding is equally delicious reheated the next day. Dulse may replace the sea lettuce if preferred.

Ingredients (serves 4):
5 g fresh sea lettuce, very finely chopped
50 g butter
75 g dark chocolate
2 large eggs
75 g sea lettuce sugar (tsp dried sea lettuce mixed with the caster sugar)
50 g plain flour
Butter for greasing

Preheat the oven to 180 °C / Gas 4. Melt the butter and chocolate in a heatproof bowl over a pan of simmering water. In a second bowl whisk the eggs and sugar together until pale and the whisk leaves a trail when lifted from the bowl. Fold the chocolate, flour and fresh sea lettuce into the whisked egg and sugar, and divide the mixture between 4 greased ramekin dishes. Pop the ramekins on a tray and bake in the oven for 10 minutes. Remove from the oven, run a knife around the edge of the ramekins and invert the puddings onto a serving dish. Serve with Chantilly sea lettuce cream or crème fraiche.

ROASTED RHUBARB AND DULSE

Slow cooking releases the aromatic flavour of rhubarb and the dulse adds umami.

Ingredients (serves 4):
4 tbsps fresh dulse, very finely chopped
Heaped tsp dried dulse, finely chopped
450 g young red rhubarb stalks (even thickness)
85 g dulse sugar to taste

Set the oven to 160 °C / Gas 3. Make the dulse sugar by briefly liquidising the granulated sugar with a heaped teaspoon of dried dulse. Wash and trim the rhubarb and cut it into 3-4 cm pieces.

Rhubarb and dulse

Cranberry and orange carrageen pudding

Put the damp rhubarb in a shallow ovenproof dish, sprinkle with dulse sugar and scatter the fresh dulse over the top. Loosely cover the dish with foil and cook in a preheated oven for 30 minutes. Remove the foil and cook for a further 5 minutes or until the rhubarb is tender but retains its shape.

DESSERTS: COLD

CRANBERRY AND ORANGE CARRAGEEN PUDDING

I made this pudding over the festive period using up leftover cranberry sauce. However it works equally well with puréed and sweetened summer fruits, or in autumn, blackberry and apple purée. Carrageen dries well and is one of my stalwart store cupboard ingredients.

Ingredients (serves 4, suitable for vegans)
15 g carrageen, rehydrated
400 ml coconut milk
200 ml soya or almond milk
2-3 tsps caster sugar (to taste – vanilla sugar works)
3 tbsp cranberry and orange sauce

Rehydrate the carrageen by soaking it in a small bowl of cold water. Put the rinsed and towel patted dry carrageen into a pan with the coconut and soya (or almond) milk. Heat over a low heat and simmer for 15 minutes until the carrageen is very soft. Strain the milk through a sieve into a large jug, using the back of a spoon to push as much of the natural carrageen gel through. Add two or three teaspoons of sugar to taste and stir to dissolve the sugar.

Line a 600 ml mould with cling film. Put the cranberry and orange sauce into the base of the mould. Pour the carrageen mixture into the lined mould and refrigerate until set. Turn the mould onto a plate and serve

Lime Jelly

This simple recipe is my version of a Hebridean pudding which was served when 'bairns' were feeling unwell. My friend Christopher Sleight said that it tastes of gooseberries. Don't miss out on the washing-up because washing the carrageen pan will soften your hands. I like the natural colour of carrageen, but some may prefer a green, lime jelly. For a rose jelly, simmer the carrageen and water with 2 handfuls of unsprayed pink rose petals (frozen petals aid the dyeing process) and add drops of rosewater to taste.

Ingredients (serves 4):
15 g dried carrageen
50 g caster sugar (to taste)
Juice of 2 limes
4-5 drops of green food colouring (optional)

Soak the carrageen in a small bowl of water for about 10 minutes to rehydrate. Rinse well under running cold water. Put the carrageen into a pan and add water to cover. Bring the pan to the boil and simmer until the water is very thick and gel like (20 minutes). Strain the thick (purple/brown) liquid into a bowl and whilst it is still hot dissolve the sugar in the gel, and then add the lime juice. Whisk well. If you are adding food colouring, do so now. Leave to set.

Pomegranate and Sea Lettuce Sorbet

This ruby red and speckled emerald jewel sorbet is a refreshing dessert after a rich main course.

Ingredients (serves 4-6):
1 tbsp dried finely chopped sea lettuce
200 g caster sugar

125 ml water
600 ml pomegranate juice
100 g pomegranate seeds (optional)

Put the sea lettuce, caster sugar and water in a pan over a low heat and cook until the sugar has dissolved. Boil briefly until you have thick syrup. Cool completely.

Add the pomegranate juice to the cooled sea lettuce and sugar syrup and mix well. Pour into an ice cream maker* and churn until frozen. Serve the jewelled sorbet scattered with fresh pomegranate seeds.

*Alternatively, put the ice cream into a freezer-safe container and freeze until slushy. Return the mixture to the bowl beat well (or whizz in a food processor) and return to the freezer. Repeat this process until you can't see any icy shreds and then freeze until frozen.

SEA-BUCKTHORN POSSET

Lady Macbeth drugged the posset of Duncan's sleeping guards, but this tart posset is delicious.

Ingredients (serves 6):
Coastal plant: 100 ml sea-buckthorn juice
500 ml double cream
125 g caster sugar (to taste)

To make sea-buckthorn juice, cook washed berries (ensuring none are over ripe) in a pan with minimal water, over a low heat until the berries break down. Push the berries through a fine plastic sieve into a jug. The more water the berries are cooked in, the thinner the juice. Sea-buckthorn berries are rich in nutrients.

Put the cream and caster sugar into a heavy-based saucepan and cook over a low heat until the sugar dissolves. Just below boiling point, remove the pan from the heat. Allow the cream to cool slightly and then whisk in the sea buckthorn juice (it will thicken). Pour the posset into small pots (it is rich, so serve small portions). Leave to cool and then refrigerate.

SEA LETTUCE ICE-CREAM

Ingredients (serves 4-6)
350 ml milk
150 ml double cream
75 g sugar
8 g carrageen (dried)
3 level teaspoons finely ground sea lettuce

Pop all of the ingredients except one teaspoon of the sea lettuce in a pan, bring to the boil and simmer for fifteen minutes. Strain through a fine sieve into a jug and add the third teaspoon of sea lettuce. Turn into an ice-cream maker and churn until frozen. Or put the ice-cream into a freezer-safe container and freeze until slushy. Return the mixture to the bowl, beat well, and then return to the freezer. Repeat this process twice and then freeze until frozen. Leave for ten minutes at room temperature before serving.

BAKING: SWEET

CHOCOLATE LAVER BITES
This recipe is by Jade Mellor, a professional forager from Wales.

Ingredients (makes 25 depending on size):
3 heaped tsps dried, toasted, crumbled laver
125 g raisins
125 g ground almonds
25 g desiccated coconut

2 tbsp maple syrup
25 g cocoa powder, sifted
Extra sifted cocoa powder for dusting

Finely chop the raisins in a food processor. Add the other ingredients, one ingredient at a time, adding the maple syrup last. You will have a slightly sticky mixture, which holds together when squeezed. Roll into walnut size balls, dust in cocoa powder and eat.

To make by hand (ideal for children), chop the raisins with a knife and put them into a large bowl. Add the other ingredients and mix together with a spoon. Roll into small balls and dip each ball into a bowl of sifted cocoa to finish.

LAVER CLOUDS

A rather subtle taste of the sea replaces the traditional chewy rice paper in this simple recipe for English macaroons. The laver will roast as it cooks.

Ingredients (makes 8):
2-3 tsps dried laver
Large egg white
50 g ground almonds
50 g caster sugar
Almond flakes to decorate

Set the oven to 180 °C / Gas 4. Line a baking sheet with baking paper. Using a 6 cm circular cutter as a template, finely scatter the laver to make 8 bases to pile with macaroon mixture. In a bowl whisk the egg white until it forms peaks and fold in the ground almonds and caster sugar. Divide the mixture between the laver bases and decorate each macaroon with a flaked almond. Bake in a preheated oven for 12-15 minutes or until firm and golden. Remove from the oven and when cool remove from the tray.

Mermaid Biscuits

Gutweed doesn't sound very appetising, but it is also called sea grass or mermaid's hair. You could use a seaweed or fish template or cutter to make these buttery biscuits which have a hint of the sea.

Ingredients (makes 15 depending on size):
3 tsps dried gutweed (to taste)
125 g unsalted butter
75 g caster sugar
180 g plain flour
Egg yolk

Set the oven to 180 ºC / Gas 4. In a mixing bowl cream the butter and sugar together. Add the flour and gutweed and bind the mixture together with the egg yolk. Work the dough together and divide in half. Roll into two 15 cm x 3 cm rolls and wrap each roll in cling film. Refrigerate for a minimum of 20 minutes (so that it is firm to slice).

Cut 1 cm slices, mark each biscuit with the back of a fork, and lay them on a non-stick-baking sheet. Bake in a preheated oven for about 12 minutes until the biscuits are golden. Keep a watchful eye because they'll brown quickly. Remove from the oven and leave to harden for 2-3 minutes before putting them on a cooling rack. Store in an airtight tin.

Laver Rockies

Adding laver, which attaches itself to a seaside rock, makes adding seaweed to a rock cake seems rather appropriate. Children love sprinkles and dried laver works well.

Ingredients (makes 6-8):
2 tbsps laver, dried and ground
225 g self raising flour

Mermaid biscuits

1 tsp baking powder
110 g butter small cubes
50 g caster sugar
100 g dried fruit
Large egg beaten
100 ml milk
1-2 tsps dried, finely ground laver for sprinkling

Set the oven to 180 ºC / Gas 4. Put the flour, baking powder and butter into a bowl and use your fingertips to mix the two together. Add the sugar, fruit and 2 tablespoons of laver and mix well with a wooden spoon. Mix in the beaten egg and enough milk to leave a thick mixture. Make 6-8 rocky heaps on a lined or greased baking tray and sprinkle ground laver over the top. Bake in a preheated oven for 15-20 minutes until golden. Cool on a wire rack.

BAKING: SAVOURY

CHARD, DULSE AND CHEESE TWISTS

This racing green dough, which is chipped with dulse, is simple to make and very versatile. Remember, a red seaweed dulse turns green when cooked. Large twists work well in picnic baskets and smaller delicate twists are useful as party dippers. When cut into biscuits the cooked dough is handy for a lunch box. For extra sea flavour and colour, add finely ground sea lettuce to the egg wash.

Ingredients (makes 15 large twists or 25 biscuits):
20 g fresh dulse, finely chopped
110 g cheese finely grated
110 g butter cut into small cubes
225 g plain flour
2 chard leaves, washed, dried, finely chopped
Lightly beaten egg
Extra flour

Set the oven to 200 ºC / Gas 6. Prepare two baking trays. Put the cheese, butter, flour, chard and dulse into a bowl (or food processor) and work together to make dough. Turn onto a lightly floured surface and knead briefly. Roll the dough into a rectangle about ½ cm thick and cut 20 x 1.5 cm lengths. Twist the straws 2-3 times as you lay them on a prepared baking tray(s). Brush with egg-wash and bake in a preheated oven for about 8-10 minutes until golden. Remove the tray(s) from the oven and transfer to a wire rack to cool. Store in an airtight tin for up to 3 days.

DULSE SCONES

Scones can be made and baked within minutes. Fresh dulse adds texture and a smoky bacon flavour without the need to wash a grill pan. The buttermilk glaze adds a golden hue to the scones. Buttermilk can be made by souring milk with lemon juice or sorrel.

Ingredients (makes 8):
15 g fresh dulse finely chopped
225 g self raising flour
1 tsp baking powder
25 g cold butter
150 ml buttermilk
Extra flour

Set the oven to 220 ºC / Gas 7. Prepare a baking tray. Sift the flour and baking powder into a bowl. Rub in the butter until the mix resembles breadcrumbs. Add the chopped dulse and mix. Stir in enough buttermilk to make dough. Turn the dough on to a lightly floured surface and gently roll to 3 cm thick. Use a 6 cm cutter to cut 8 scones from the dough. Put the scones onto the prepared baking tray, glaze with buttermilk and bake in a preheated oven for 10 minutes until the scones are risen and golden. Cool on a wire rack.

Pizza Dough

The addition of any finely ground dried seaweed species – such as finely chopped fresh dulse, sea spaghetti, *ulva spp*, green sponge fingers or sugar kelp – is pizza or pasta dough friendly.

Ingredients (makes 2 x 23 cm pizza bases):
1 heaped tsp dried seaweed of your choice eg. sea lettuce
225 g strong plain flour
1 tsp fast action dried yeast
½ tsp sugar
1 tbsp olive oil
150 ml tepid water
Extra flour for kneading

Add the sea lettuce to 150 ml of boiling water and leave to cool until it is blood warm. Put the flour, yeast, sugar and oil in a bowl and add enough warm sea lettuce water to mix into a dough. Turn the dough onto a lightly floured surface and knead until the dough is elastic (about 10 minutes). Put the dough into a lightly greased bowl, cover with a plastic bag and leave until it has doubled in size (about an hour). The dough is ready to be used as a pizza base.

Rock Samphire Water Biscuits

These biscuits taste almost floral with a salty hint of the sea. Dried seaweed could replace the rock samphire and either ingredient may be added to an oatcake recipe.

Rock samphire water biscuits

Shony breadsticks

Ingredients (makes 30 depending on size):
Coastal plant: 2 heaped tsps finely ground dried rock samphire seeds
200 g sifted plain flour
75 g cold butter, small cubed
40 ml iced water

Set the oven to 160 ºC / Gas 4. In a bowl (or food processor) mix the flour and butter together and add enough iced water to make dough. On a lightly floured surface roll the dough to a rectangle about 50 cm x 25 cm. Brush the dough with iced water and scatter a teaspoon of the ground rock samphire seeds over the surface. Fold the dough into three (as in puff pastry) and roll out again. Repeat. Scatter the second teaspoon of rock samphire seeds over the surface and roll over the seeds. Roll out the dough as thinly as possible. (The thinner the dough, the more 'cracker like' it will be. You will also benefit from a greater biscuit yield and faster cooking time.) Lightly brush the pastry with iced water and use a small cutter to stamp out biscuits. Prick the biscuits with a fork to prevent rising. Place the biscuits on trays lined with baking paper and bake for 10-12 minutes in a preheated oven until a pale golden. The water biscuits will harden when cold. Transfer to a wire rack to cool. Store in an airtight tin.

SHONY BREADSTICKS

Shony was the sea god Outer Hebrideans bribed with ale, in anticipation of a bountiful seaweed harvest. Shony breadsticks are delicious dipped in a boiled egg.

Ingredients (makes ten 20 cm bread sticks):
1 heaped tsp finely ground dried pepper dulse.
300 g strong white flour
2 tsps dried yeast
1 dstspn olive oil
Large pinch sugar
Approx 175 ml tepid water
Extra flour
Extra olive oil
Extra pepper dulse for dusting

Set the oven to 200 °C / Gas 6. Lightly flour two baking trays. Whisk the finely heaped teaspoon of ground pepper dulse in 175 ml of tepid water. Put the flour in a mixing bowl with the yeast, dessertspoon of olive oil and sugar. Add pepper dulse infused water to form dough and knead until the dough is elastic (about 10 minutes). Divide the dough into 10 and roll into pencil shapes (18-20 cm). Place 5 sticks on each tray, leaving space in between. Cover with a plastic bag and leave to rise in a warm place for 30 minutes. Roll the sticks briefly to ensure that they haven't stuck to the tin and then use a pastry brush to lightly brush each stick with olive oil. Sprinkle ground pepper dulse over the oiled dough and turn and repeat for the other side. Bake in a preheated oven for 12-15 minutes (depending on size) until the breadsticks are golden brown. Remove the tray from the oven and set on a wire rack to cool.

Seaweed Starter (for Sourdough)

When I read that the biblical botanists Dr Harold Moldenke and his wife Alma noted that a dried species of seaweed might have been one of the three descriptions of manna mentioned in the Bible, I was inspired to experiment with seaweed and wholemeal flour as a natural leaven. I have made dulse, laver and sugar kelp seaweed starters with equal success. I include a handful of fresh, or a tablespoon of dried dulse when I make bread. Extra seaweed may be added to sourdough also.

Ingredients:
6/7 tbsps very finely chopped dried laver
Wholemeal flour
Tepid water

Day one
In a stoneware casserole dish mix 100 g flour, 2 tablespoons of dried laver and enough tepid water to make a thick batter. Cover with muslin and leave in a warm draftproof place. The exact timing varies. Fermentation may begin within a few hours or take a day.

Day two
There should be lots of bubbles, which mean that fermentation has begun. The feeding commences: Feed the starter with 100 g flour, 1 tablespoon of laver and enough tepid water to mix to a thick batter consistency. Cover and leave for 24 hours.

Day three
Discard half of the starter and add 50 g flour, 1 tablespoon of dried laver and tepid water to blend.

Laver sourdough

Seaweed breads with seaweed starter

Days four, five (and six if necessary)
Repeat as per instruction at Day three. By day five/six a thick bubbly froth, which smells pleasantly beer-like and is obviously active should have formed. This is your natural seaweed leaven and you are ready to make sourdough bread.

To halt the process, refrigerate the starter for up to a week or freeze for a longer period. The starter will reactivate on thawing. If liquid gathers on the surface (this is called a hooch and often happens if a starter is refrigerated) worry not, just stir it in. Should the sponge layer not occur, start again – harsh, but there it is.

SEAWEED SOURDOUGH

Ingredients (makes one load):
400 g strong flour
200 g active starter
1tsp salt
225 ml tepid water
Olive oil
Rice flour for dusting

Set the oven to 220 °C / Gas 7. Measure the flour onto the scales and make a well in the centre. Add the starter in the well and put the measured ingredients into a bowl. Add the salt and enough water to make wet dough. Knead for 10-15 minutes until the dough is elastic and when held up to the light and pulled, there is a see-through windowpane. Put the dough into a lightly oiled bowl, cover with a plastic bag and leave in a draftproof place until the dough has doubled in size. Knock the dough back briefly and put the dough in a well rice-floured banneton or proving basket. Cover and leave until well risen.

Put a small tray of water and a baking tray in a preheated oven. Remove the baking tray, lightly dust it with rice flour and turn the sourdough onto the tray. Slash the top of the loaf 3-4 times with a sharp knife and put the bread in the oven. Bake for 18 minutes and lower the temperature to 200 °C / Gas 6, remove the water and bake for a further 8-10 minutes until the base is hollow when tapped. For a soft crust, wrap the hot bread in a clean tea-towel.

SAUCES

SEA-BUCKTHORN *BEURRE BLANC*

Sea-buckthorn juice has an oily feel to it and this, coupled with its sharpness, encouraged the development of this *beurre blanc* recipe. Its perfection must be credited to my Goddaughter Lucie's, mother Nici and her excellent partner Ronnie. The sauce is delicious with shellfish.

Ingredients:
Coastal plant: 100 g sea-buckthorn berries, washed
50 ml water
1dsp finely chopped shallot
Zest and juice ½ small lime
150 g butter, cubed
½ tsp light brown sugar
Additional lime juice and black pepper

Put the berries and water into a pan on a low heat and cook until the berries burst. Push the berries through a plastic sieve and reserve the juice. Heat a knob of the butter in a pan and sauté the shallot briefly. Add the lime zest and sea-buckthorn juice and boil to reduce by half. Lower the heat and slowly whisk in the butter and sugar until you have a glossy sauce. Sieve to remove the shallots and lime zest (if desired) and add lime juice and black pepper to taste. Keep the *beurre blanc* warm until use, but protect it from fierce, direct heat or it may split.

Sea Oak Caramel Sauce

This is an adaptation of a sea lettuce caramel recipe in my book, *The Forager's Kitchen*. Sea oak has a nutty taste and is delicious trickled over ice-cream or used as the base to a sponge pudding. This can be made with any species of dried ground seaweed.

Ingredients (makes 300 ml):
2 heaped tsps dried and finely ground sea oak
175 ml double cream
150 ml water
300 g caster sugar

Measure the cream into a pan and add a teaspoon of sea oak. Stir and bring to just below boiling point and set aside. Put the water in a heavy-based pan and add the sugar and remaining teaspoon of sea oak. Try not to let the sugar touch the sides of the pan – I use a wide frying pan. Dissolve the sugar as slowly as possible on a low heat. Increase the heat and simmer until the sugar begins to caramelise – this will take 15-20 minutes. Stir occasionally but keep a watchful eye on the pan. When the sugar begins to brown do not stir, but 'shuggle' the pan to ensure even heat distribution. When the caramel is golden remove the pan from the heat and quickly add the prepared sea oak cream – stand back because the caramel will splutter. Stir vigorously to mix in the cream. Cool for a few minutes and pour into a jug and serve hot with ice cream or comfort puddings. Alternatively pour into a jam jar, cover when cold and refrigerate for 2-3 weeks.

MISCELLANEOUS

Kelp Stipes

I was convinced that kelp stipes were going to be the winter sea edible, my island answer to storm-cancelled ferries. We ate lots. Success is along the lines of 'Small kelp stipe is beautiful and don't be too greedy'. Our preference in descending order is dabberlocks, sugar kelp, oarweed and forest kelp. We didn't trial furbellows.

Ingredients (serves 4):
200 g kelp stipes no more than 1 cm in width
Seawater

Cut the stipes into 1-2 cm lengths, wrap in greaseproof paper and place in a pressure cooker steamer. Fill the steamer a quarter full with seawater and bring the pan up to pressure. Follow the manufacturer's instruction for releasing pressure. My WMF pressure cooker didn't give seaweed guidelines but by trial and error I found that it took 45 minutes cooking time for most kelp stipes to become palatable. Kelp stipe is delicious in a spicy tomato sauce; seaweed purists might prefer to add a sprinkling of finely ground bladder wrack, which works well with flavoursome tomatoes.

BEETROOT AND SUGAR KELP DUST

Dried beetroot and kelp dust adds flavour to soups, casseroles, stir-fries, crumbles, and muffins. A colourful idea is to serve a small pot of the beetroot and sugar kelp dust with boiled quail eggs, in much the same way that celery salt is served. It also provides flavour and colour contrast, for example to mashed avocado on bruschetta (see recipe on page 155). This recipe may be adapted to use other root and sea vegetables. The drying process could also take place in a low oven.

Ingredients (makes 1 small jar):
150 g sugar kelp fronds
5 small beetroots

Wash the beetroots and bake or boil them, as you prefer. If possible cool them over a bowl of ice to reduce the temperature as soon as possible. Remove the skin and cut the cooled beetroots as finely as possible using a mandoline slicer.

Spread the evenly sized slices over food dehydrator trays (or on baking trays in a low oven). Set the temperature to 70 °C (high) and dehydrate for an hour and then reduce the temperature to 50 °C and dehydrate overnight (or to manufacturer's instruction) until the beetroot slices are brittle. The final colour of the beetroots is dependent on the drying temperature, and in my experience the lower the sequential heat temperature the better the colour preservation.

Cut the sugar kelp fronds into lengths of the same size and dry at 70 °C for 30 minutes and then for a further 2-3 hours at 45 °C until the kelp is completely dry and crumbles with ease. Put the dried beetroot and kelp into a grinder and blend until finely ground.

RHUBARB AND DULSE SMOOTHIE

Finely chopped dulse adds volume to milk when blended. Drink the smoothie quickly before the magic disappears.

Ingredients (serves 1):
2 tbsps prepared cold roasted rhubarb and dulse (page 198)
2 tbsps Greek yoghurt
100 ml milk
Honey (optional)

In a liquidiser, blend the cold rhubarb and dulse with the Greek yoghurt. Add enough milk to dilute the smoothie to desired consistency (approx 100 ml). Add honey to taste.

FERMENTED DULSE, CARROT AND NETTLE TOPS

Gut-enriching fermented food is not to everyone's taste but I was keen to experiment with seaweed. A reaction using fresh sugar kelp appears to be faster than dulse, but the pink pigment from red seaweed gives the fermenting liquid a wonderful pink hue.

Ingredients (makes 1 jar):
2 heaped tbsps fresh dulse finely chopped
2 handfuls nettle tops
1 large carrot peeled and sliced.
1 tsp finely chopped red chilli
2 tsps sea salt (ideally home dried infused with dulse)

Blanch the nettle tops and refresh in cold water. Layer the dulse and nettle tops into a large jam jar and pack the sliced carrot on top. Grind the finely chopped chilli and sea salt in a pestle and mortar to make a paste and dissolve this in 250 ml water.

Add the chilli salt water to the jar and swill the jug out with more water to cover the root, leaf and sea vegetables. Cover with a double layer of parchment paper or a coffee filter and secure with an elastic band to prevent the vegetables from floating and put an airtight lid on the jar. Leave for a week, shaking daily.

Taste and leave the vegetables to ferment for longer if it isn't sour to your palate. When the vegetables are pleasantly sour, refrigerate. Serve the fermented vegetables as you would a pickle, or use them in tortilla wraps or sandwiches. Forgotten jars may develop mould, but just scrape it off and see what is underneath. A pleasant sour smell gets the thumbs up.

FERMENTED CARROT STICKS
This is a great lunchbox or snack idea.

Ingredients:
4 tbsps chopped, fresh dulse
Approx 3 carrots, peeled and cut into sticks/batons
Brine

To make brine I use one heaped tablespoon of seaweed infused salt to 250 ml tepid water. The exact amount of brine and carrots needed will depend on the size of the jar. Pop the chopped dulse in a jar. Add the carrot sticks and pour in the brine. Cover with greaseproof paper or a coffee filter, and secure with an elastic band. Leave the carrot sticks to ferment. This can take from three days to three weeks depending on your palate. Seal with an airlocked lid, label and refrigerate.

Pepper Dulse Syrup

This rather quirky flavoured syrup can be adapted to use dulse or kelp. If using kelp, simmer it in hot water for 30 minutes before use. Some might say that pepper dulse should be married with fish, or used in a condiment, because of its pungent taste but I disagree. The syrup is sweet but subtly fiery in a peppery kind of way. It is delicious with finely sliced tart grapefruits and blood oranges.

Ingredients (makes a small jug):
5 g dried pepper dulse
300 ml boiling water
Caster sugar

Put the pepper dulse and boiling water in a bowl and leave for an hour. Strain the liquid through muslin or a fine sieve into a measuring jug. For each ml add 2 g of caster sugar i.e. for 125 ml use 250 g sugar. Put the liquid and sugar into a pan and cook over a low heat to dissolve the sugar and then boil rapidly for 2-3 minutes until you have a thick syrup.

Pickled Marsh Samphire

Sea aster and marsh samphire often grow within feet of each other, so I was encouraged to combine them. This recipe may also be used for sea aster buds but only pick them where they grow prolifically. Pickled sea aster buds may replace capers in a sauce tartare.

Ingredients (makes 2 small jars):
150 g well washed marsh samphire
225 ml sea aster vinegar
2-3 mustard seeds per jar
1 coriander seed per jar
2 pink peppercorn seeds per jar
Pinch of mace per jar

Cook the well-washed marsh samphire in a pan of boiling water for a minute and then refresh in a bowl of iced water. Drain well and remove excess water by gently wrapping the blanched samphire in a tea towel. Roughly chop the samphire and pack it with the spices in small sterile jars. Top up the jars with sea aster vinegar. Seal with a vinegar proof lid and store in a cool, dark place shaking the jar gently when you come across it. This is delicious served as a tracklement with smoked fish or cheese.

SEA SALT

Sea salt is easy to make. The kitchen may become rather steamy in the process but the resulting sea salt is delicious, and of course free. It is a great activity to do with children and older ones may learn a little saline science too. On the beach fill a container with seawater and on returning to the kitchen filter the water through a jelly bag. Put the strained water in a wide shallow pan and heat until the water has evaporated and crystals (salt) have formed on the base of the pan. Use a spatula to remove the salt and finish the drying process in a low oven 120 °C / Gas ½. To make seaweed infused salt, add seaweed to the strained seawater. Tiny pepper dulse fronds add a piquant flavour. Alternatively add finely ground dried seaweed to home dried or shop sea salt.

SEA ASTER BUTTER

This versatile butter can be used to sauté shellfish and vegetables or in a roux for a fish sauce. Sea aster leaves are often served wilted in garlic butter and you might like to add garlic to this recipe, but I prefer to allow the flavour of the sea aster to shine through. Sea aster leaves retain their texture during cooking. Seaweed butter may be made in the same way by replacing the sea aster leaves with finely chopped, fresh or dried seaweed to taste.

Ingredients:
50 g sea aster leaves, finely chopped
125 g soft unsalted butter

Put the butter into a bowl and beat with a wooden spoon. Add the chopped leaves and work the two ingredients together. This can be done in a food processor, but take care not to cut the leaves too finely or the result will be a green mess. Lay a small rectangle of cling film on a work surface and heap the mashed butter in a line down the centre. Use the cling film to roll the butter into a sausage shape about 3-4 cm in diameter. Knot each end of excess cling film and refrigerate or freeze until use.

SEA ASTER VINEGAR

Edible coastal flowers and fruits add flavour to homemade vinegars. Sea rocket flowers turn rice vinegar pink, but the flavour from sea aster is more delicate. Coastal floral vinegars may be used in pavlova, vinaigrettes, or added to sparkling water as a drink. It also lends itself as a base to pickled quail eggs.

Ingredients (makes 1 small jar):
7 g (3 tbsp) sea aster petals
250 ml rice or white wine vinegar

Put the sea aster petals (having removed any green bits) into

225

a sterile jar with a non-metallic lid (vinegar proof). Heat the vinegar in a stainless steel pan or in a glass jug in the microwave until it is warm. Do not boil.

Pour the warm vinegar over the flowers and leave the vinegar to cool before sealing with a non-metallic lid. Leave for 3-4 weeks for the flavour to infuse and then strain into a clean jar. Seal with a vinegar proof lid.

SEA-BUCKTHORN CURD

Ingredients (makes 3-4 small jars):
200 g sea-buckthorn berries, washed
Heaped tsp finely chopped sea-buckthorn leaves
50 ml water
125 g butter
350 g sugar
3 eggs and 2 additional yolks, lightly beaten

Put the sea-buckthorn berries and water in a pan and simmer until soft (5 minutes). Push the liquid and berries through a sieve into a large, heat resistant bowl. There will be about 100 ml of thick juice. Put the bowl over a pan of simmering water. Add the butter and sugar to the sea-buckthorn juice and stir until the sugar has dissolved and butter melted. Quickly whisk in the beaten eggs and yolks and sea-buckthorn leaves, and continue to cook until the mixture thickens (coats the back of the wooden spoon). Pour the curd into warm, dry sterilized jars, cool, seal and label. Refrigerate and use within 2 weeks.

SCENTED PICKLED KELP STIPES

The cardamom adds a flowery tang, one which Victorian collectors of seaweed might have appreciated, although perhaps in a nosegay or herbarium rather than on a plate.

Pickled kelp stipes may be added to chutneys and savoury dishes. You may like to experiment with fragrant vinegars. Elderflower vinegar works well. However, kelp stipes sweeten as they age. When I prepared a seaweed smorgasbord on the stunning Luskentyre beach on the West coast of the Isle of Harris for BBC Scotland, the programme's presenter, Mark Stephens, commented that the stipe would be delicious with ice-cream. The stipe was a three-year vintage and had benefitted from time to mature.

Ingredients (makes 1 small jar):

125 g 1 cm (thin) kelp lengths cooked

2 tsps caster sugar

25 mls Mirin

75 mls white wine vinegar

½ tsp caraway seeds

½ tsp coriander seeds

½ tsp mace

4-5 peppercorns

¼ star anise

3 cardamom seeds, lightly crushed

Cook the kelp in a pressure cooker and immediately refresh in iced water. Put all the other ingredients (apart from the kelp) in a small stainless steel pan (or a microwave-proof jug) and heat on the hob (or microwave) for 2-4 minutes to dissolve the sugar. Leave to cool completely. Put the kelp in a sterile jar(s) and pour the pickling liquid into the jar. The kelp will sink, leaving about 2 cm of pickling liquid at the top of the jar.

Don't be tempted to add more kelp because the lengths, with time, will distribute evenly. Seal the jar with a non-metallic vinegar-proof lid and leave in a cool dark place for at least 6 weeks before using. Shake the jar when you remember to.

Simple Clear Seaweed Stock

Dashi is a very important component of Japanese cooking used in soups, stews, when cooking vegetables, and in an assortment of other ways. It is traditionally made with sun-dried kelp and bonito that has been dried and shaved into small slivers.

Some Japanese cooks now use powdered *dashi,* but it has added MSG to enhance the umami wow, and is frowned upon by purists. After reading about *kombu dashi,* which is in essence kelp stock, and with the knowledge that vegans use *kombu* and water, I decided to experiment. My favourite seaweeds to use for stock are sugar kelp and dulse. Dulse has the added advantage of a red pigment that is soluble in water. Pepper dulse when soaked in water will also turn stock a shade of pink. It has a less subtle flavour than dulse, but when you need a piquant stock this is the seaweed to use. Sometimes dulse stock is red and at others only slightly tinted. Professor Guiry suggested that the red pigment, (phycoerythrin) in red seaweeds might be degraded when it is dried.

Dulse that has been frozen usually produces red stock. Whatever the colour, seaweed stock is a delicious base for any vegetarian, fish or chicken risotto.

Ingredients (makes 1 litre):
25 cm frond sugar kelp, washed
1 litre cold water

Use scissors to make half a dozen incisions into the sugar kelp at various intervals and then put the sugar kelp and water into a pan and leave it to soak for at least 30 minutes. Put the pan on the hob and bring to the boil over a very low heat. Do this as slowly as possible to allow the flavour to infuse. Remove the sugar kelp at the point of boil for a milder stock or for a stronger stock leave the frond in the stock until it is cold. Store

Pickled kelp

sugar kelp stock for up to three days or freeze for later use. If I make this with dried seaweed, I leave the seaweed to soak in the water overnight.

Sugar Kelp and Gammon Scratchings

Even if you ensure that most of the fat is removed from the gammon, it won't make this a very healthy snack.

Ingredients (makes a small bowl depending on size of the rind):
4 pieces fresh sugar kelp, slightly larger than the rind and as dry as possible
Gammon rind (see 2 kg gammon recipe on page 183)

Set the oven to 180 °C / Gas 4. Scrape excess fat from the gammon rind and then put two pieces of sugar kelp underneath the rind and two on top, and wrap the sugar kelp tightly around the rind. Wrap the sugar kelp encased rind tightly in baking paper and then in foil. Put the package on a baking tray and cook in a preheated oven for 1-1 ½ hours until the rind is golden and crispy. Remove the foil and paper and allow the scratchings to cool before breaking into bite-sized pieces.

Sugar Kelp Crisps

Ingredients:
Decent lengths of fresh sugar kelp, 30 to 40 cm
Vegetable oil
Nigella seeds

Use a pastry brush to coat both sides of the sugar kelp with oil (generously). Pop it on a baking tray in the preheated oven to

160 ºC / Gas 4 for 8-10 minutes until the seaweed turns green. Remove from the oven.

Turn the frond and coat with additional oil and sprinkle the upper side with Nigella seeds. Return to the oven and cook until crisp (this will depend on the thickness of the sugar kelp). Break into crisps and serve.

Delesseria sanguinea (Sea Beech)

PICTURE CREDITS

Fiona Bird: photographs on front cover and pages 2, 8, 18, 22, 33, 40, 44, 47, 52, 57, 59, 63, 65, 67, 69, 71, 72, 73, 75, 77, 78, 84, 86, 111, 154, 157, 179, 185, 193, 195, 199, 200, 207, 211, 212, 215, 216, 229.
Jhonti Bird: table on page 25.
Dr Olivia Bird: tables on pages 27, 28.
Professor Mike Guiry: photographs on pages 59, 78.
Sarah Hotchkiss table on page 151.
Peter Moore: author photograph on back cover
The Wellcome Collection: photograph on page 146.
Wikipedia: photographs on pages 90, 105.

Background on front cover is by William Kilburn, V & A.

Image of *Chorda filum* on page 117 by kind permission of the Herbarium (STA), St Andrews Botanic Garden Trust.

Special thanks to Elizabeth Twelvetree for the seaweed illustrations on the back cover and on pages 1, 21, 30, 48, 102, 128, 231.

General references

Abbott, Isabella A. & Bangmei Xia. 'Edible Seaweeds of China and Their Place in the Chinese Diet', *Economic Botany*, Vol. 41, No. 3 (Jul-Sep 1987):341-35.

Allom, Elizabeth Anne. *Sea-side Pleasures; or, A Peep at Miss Eldon's Happy Pupils*, Aylott and Jones, 1845.

Barber, Lynn. *The Heyday of Natural History*, Doubleday & Company, 1980.

Beith, Mary. *Healing Threads: Traditional Medicines of the Highlands and Islands*, Birlinn Ltd, 2004.

Bird, Isabella, *Korea and Her Neighbours*, New York: Fleming Revell, 1897.

Bunker, Francis, Juliet Brodie, Christine Maggs & Anne Bunker. *Seaweeds of Britain and Ireland*, Wild Nature Press, 2012.

Carson, Rachael. *The Edge of the Sea*, Mariner Books, 1998.

Chapman, V.J. *Seaweeds and Their Uses*, Camelot Press, 1950.

Cheape, Jane. *Hand to Mouth: The Traditional Food of the Scottish Islands*, Acair, 2002.

Christie, Ann. 'A Taste for Seaweed: William Kilburn's Late Eighteenth-Century Designs for Printed Cottons,' *Journal of Design History*, Vol. 24, No. 4 (2011):299-314.

Clarke, Lousia Lane. *Common Seaweeds of the British coast and Channel Islands*, Frederick Warne, 1865.

Darwin, Tess. *The Scots Herbal: The Plant Lore of Scotland*, Mercat Press, 1996.

Dickinson, Carola I. *British Seaweeds*, Eyre & Spottiswoode, 1963.

Ellis, Lesley. *Simply Seaweed*, Grub Street, 1998.

Gatty, Mrs Margaret. *British Sea-Weeds* Vol 1 & Vol 2, London: Bell and Daldy, 1872.

Gibbons, Euell. *Stalking the Blue-Eyed Scallop*, Alan C Hood and Co, 1964.

Grieve, Mrs M. *A Modern Herbal*, Tiger Books International/Cressset Press, 1992.

Hardy, FG, Guiry, MD. *A Check-list and Atlas of the Seaweeds of Britain and Ireland*, The British Phycological Society, 2003,1-50.

Hartley, Dorothy. *Food in England*, Little Brown & Co, 1999.

Hartley, Dorothy. *The Countryman's England*, Little Brown & Co, 1999.

Harvey, William Henry. *A Manual of the British Marine Algae*, J. Van Voorst, 1849.

Houston, Fiona & Xa Milne. *Seaweed and Eat It: A Family Foraging and Cooking Adventure*, Virgin Books 2008.

Major, Alan. *The Book of Seaweed*, Gordon & Cremonesi, 1977.

Martynoga, Fi. *A Handbook of Scotland's Wild Harvests*, Saraband, 2012.

Maxwell, Christabel. *Mrs Gatty and Mrs Ewing*, Constable, 1947.

McKenna, Sally. *Extreme Greens: Understanding Seaweeds*, Estragon Press, 2013.

Miller, Francine Koslow. 'Michael Silver's Sushi Prints: 47 Variations on a Sheet of Nori Seaweed', *The Print Collector's Newsletter*, Vol. 24, No. 2 (May-June 1993): 41-44.

Milne, Xa. *The Seaweed Cookbook*, Michael Joseph, 2016.

Mitchell, Pamela. *Edible Wild Plants and Herbs*, Grub Street Publishing, 2015.

Moore, P.G. 'Popularizing Marine Natural History in Eighteenth- and Nineteenth-Century Britain', *Archives of Natural History* Vol. 41, 1 (2014):45-62.

Mouritsen, Ole. *Seaweeds Edible, Available & Sustainable*, University of Chicago Press, 2013.

Newton, Lily (ed.). *A Handbook of the British Seaweeds*, Trustees of the British Museum, 1931.

O'Connor, Kaori. *Seaweed: A Global History*, Reaktion Books, 2017

Philips, Roger. *Seashells and Seaweeds*, Elm Tree Books, 1987.

Rhatigan, Prannie. *Irish Seaweed Kitchen*, Booklink, 2009.

Robertson, Duncan J. 'Among the Kelpers', *Longman's Magazine*, November 1895.

Robertson, John. 'The Purple Shore', *Household Words*, Vol. XIV, 1856.

Shetterly, Susan Hand. *Seaweed Chronicles: A World at the Water's Edge*, Algonquin Books, 2018.

Surey-Gent, Sonia & Gordon Morris. *Seaweed: A User's Guide*, Whittet Books, 1987.

Tilden, Josephine E. 'Our Richest Source of Vitamins', *Scientific American*, Vol. 138, No. 2 (February 1928):114-117.

Uchida, Motoharu. 'Fermentation studies for wise utilization of seaweeds', paper given at the International Seaweed Symposium, 2016.

Warwick-Evans, Caroline & Tim Van Berkel. *The Seaweed Cookbook: A Guide*. Lorenz Books, 2018.

White, Florence. *Good Things in England: A Practical Cookery Book for Everyday Use*, Persephone Books, 1999.

Wilson, M. A. 'Anne Elizabeth Ball of Youghal', *The Irish Naturalists' Journal*, Vol. 11, No. 8 (October 1954):213-215.

Wood, Elizabeth & Frances Dipper. *Sea Life of Britain & Ireland*, Immel Publishing, 1988.

Wright, John. *Edible Seashore*, Bloomsbury Publishing, 2009.

Useful websites
www.algaebase.org
www.biomara.org
www.brphycsoc.org
www.linnean.org
www.marinespecies.org/index.php
www.nhm.ac.uk/nature-online/british-natural-history/seaweeds-survey/
www.seaweed.ie/index.php
www.seaweedindustry.com
www.spnhc.org (see link, 'How to No. 2' (prepare seaweed speciments)

Seaweed courses
www.eatweeds.co.uk
www.fergustheforager.co.uk
www.foodsafari.co.uk
www.gallowaywildfoods.com
www.monicawilde.com
www.wildaboutpembrokeshire.co.uk
www.wild-food.net
www.wildpickings.co.uk

Seaweed harvesters and suppliers
www.atlantickitchen.co.uk
www.beachfood.co.uk
www.blathnamara.ie
www.cornishseaweedcompany.co.uk
www.hebrideanseaweed.co.uk
www.justseaweed.com
www.irishseaweeds.com
www.maraseaweed.com/shop
www.seaspoon.com
www.seaveg.co.uk
www.seaweedproducts.ie
Storm Kelpie Seaweed

Seaweed fed lamb producers
www.briggs-shetlandlamb.co.uk/the-product/

Seaweed-based health & skincare stockists
www.ishga.co.uk
www.seagreens.co.uk
www.seaweedorganics.co.uk